Naked Clay

CERAMICS WITHOUT GLAZE

Naked Clay

CERAMICS WITHOUT GLAZE

JANE PERRYMAN

H E R B E R T   P R E S S
LONDON · OXFORD · NEW YORK · NEW DELHI · SYDNEY

University of Pennsylvania Press • Pennsylvania

For my mother and sisters

HERBERT PRESS
Bloomsbury Publishing Plc
50 Bedford Square, London, WC1B 3DP, UK
29 Earlsfort Terrace, Dublin 2, Ireland

BLOOMSBURY, HERBERT PRESS and the
Herbert Press logo are trademarks of
Bloomsbury Publishing Plc

First published 2004 in Great Britain
by A & C Black (Publishers) Limited
This edition published in 2023

Published simultaneously in the USA by
University of Pennsylvania Press
3905 Spruce Street, Philadelphia
Pennsylvania

UK ISBN: 978-1-7899-4326-9
US ISBN: 978-0-8122-2056-8

A catalogue record for this book is available
from the British Library

To find out more about our authors and
books visit www.bloomsbury.com and sign
up for our newsletters

Cover design: Dorothy Moir
Book design: Penny and Tony Mills

Printed and bound in China by RR Donnelley
Asia Printing Solutions Limited company

COVER ILLUSTRATIONS:
(Front) *Tall Vessel* by Felicity Aylieff,
40 x 40 x 150 cm (15¾ x 15¾ x 59in.).
Photograph by Sebastian Mylius.
(Back, top) *Burnished Vessels* by Jane Perryman,
w: 39 cm (15⅜in.). Photograph by Graham Murrell.
(Back, bottom) *Burnished Vessel*, w: 40 cm
(15¾ in.), 2003. Photograph by Graham Murrell.

Contents

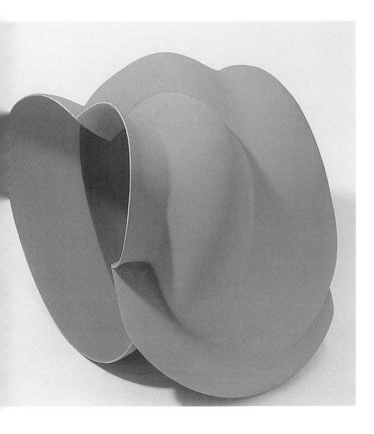

(Above) *Blue Shape* by Wouter Dam, 2001,
26 x 23cm (10¼ x 9in.).

2 Clay Marked by Fire 60

(saggar firing, smoke firing, raku firing, black firing)

3 Pure Clay 94

(clay without addition)

(Left above) *M3 Configuation* by Tjok Dessauvage.
(Left) Detail of high-fired porcelain vessels by David Jones.
Photograph by Rod Dorling.
(Opposite) Detail of *Division* by Violette Fassbaender, ht: 40cm (15 3/4 in.), l: 70cm (27½ in.).

4 Clay with Additions   136

(colouring clays, neriage, mixing clay
with aggregates and combustibles)

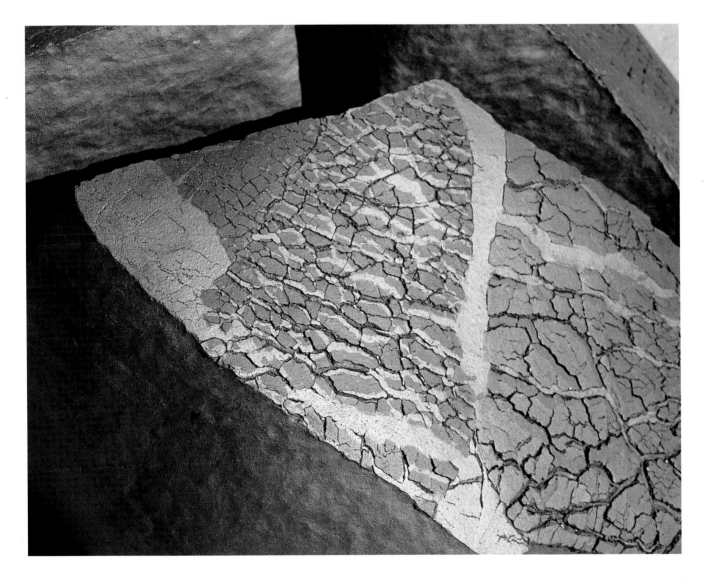

Acknowledgements

I inherited this book from Duncan Ayscough who was unable to proceed with his research due to family commitments. I would like to thank him for the generous offer of his material, which I was unable to accept in order to make it 'my book'. My research included 22 visits to the studios and homes of ceramicists I wanted to present in depth. Their hospitality and generosity with both time and material was beyond the call of duty and often entailed overnight stays with the additional bonus of their company and friendship. Thanks to all of them. Thanks also to the artists I corresponded with, some of whom I was unable to meet but who kindly sent images and information. Thanks to Moira Vincentelli who shared her historical expertise by offering suggestions for the background section and who also agreed to write the foreword. Thanks to my publisher Linda Lambert who always gives me her time and to my editor Alison Stace who I worked with on the final draft and proofs.

(Above) *Porcelain Installation* by Arnold Annen, dia: 20 cm (8 in.), 2001. Photograph by Reto Bernhardt.

Foreword

Naked Clay – the words conjure up evocatively the primal quality of the stuff of ceramics – that cool earth transformed by the heat of the flame. The product can be rough and rock-like or smooth and seductive. It can be spun from the wheel into an arrested motion leaving the sign of the spinning action. It can be polished or layered, squeezed or shaped into elegant forms and coloured to convey the harmonies of nature, or torn and distressed to suggest disharmony. For all the artists represented here it is the properties of the materials themselves that sing out.

In 1914 Clive Bell coined the expression 'Significant Form'. It became the central concept of his aesthetic theory which proposed that an appropriate emotional response to the work of art should be to the form, the colour and the abstract qualities of the work. The subject matter and narrative aspects were, in his eyes, always secondary and impure. Although such a view has long been questioned and few would accept that there can be such a radical division between form and its associations, many of the makers in this book do seem to be searching for a structural essence for which the phrase 'Significant Form' seems apt.

It is tempting to see in the work of these artists an attachment to the timeless universal ideals of modernism and the doctrine of truth to materials. Primitivism too is a source to be tapped, as it was for artists in the early 20th century. Most have rejected the complex referencing and borrowing of postmodern ironies in favour of something more elemental and sometimes minimal. Their work is serious and sober and avoids the dark humour or light-hearted whimsy that is currently so common in much contemporary art. Figurative work is also little in evidence with the exceptions of Mo Jupp and Anna Noel both of whom have an ancient feel to their sculptures.

Although, on the whole, decorative surfaces are avoided in the desire for a more profound unity of form and surface, they are not totally absent. Instead the decoration is cerebral or brain-teasing as in Elizabeth Fritsch's syncopated patterns on illusionistic forms or Lesley Thompson's optical geometries. Sometimes it is light itself that creates the pattern as in Sasha Wardell or Margaret O'Rorke's work, or fire, as illustrated in the section on 'Clay Marked by Fire'.

Many of these artists favour the simple technology of handbuilding: Elspeth Owen pinches out her pots, Lawson Oyekan builds up with wads of clay like the accretions of termite mounds. References to natural processes abound: Sara Radstone's forms seem to have been eroded through time; Yo Akiyama's re-assembled thrown cylinders suggest geological processes; Violette Fassbaender's sculptures are inspired by the Alpine scenery of her native Switzerland. Felicity Aylief's amalgamate may, in part, suggest the manufactured surface of terrazzo tile but equally can convey the mottled quality of granite moulded into organic shapes. Her sculptures could be seen as a kind of industrial equivalent of the natural forces of geology. By contrast 'naked clay' can still be applied to the cool precision of slip-cast or moulded forms and the sharp geometric shapes and rhythms to be found in the work of artists such as Dave Binns, Nicolas Rena or Tjok Dessauvage.

I am struck by the amazing internationalism of ceramic artists and the openness to the exchange of ideas: Thomas Hoadley is American but is an expert in the use of 'nerikomi', a specialist Japanese technique, Lawson Oyekan works in Britain and Jill Solomon in the USA but both draw on African roots; Violette Fassbaender from Switzerland was inspired to take up pottery in Japan, Jane Perryman herself found spiritual inspiration in India. Contemporary ceramic artists are part of a global community.

Able to explore strands of thought and pick out common concerns that touch artists from across the world, the author's interviews bring the insights of one who also struggles with the material and the process. In *Naked Clay* Jane Perryman has identified a fascinating theme that underpins a major body of work by contemporary ceramic artists.

Moira Vincentelli

Introduction

The title of this book began its life as 'Ceramics without Glaze' and through the many discussions with various ceramicists has gradually metamorphised into 'Naked Clay'. In this way it has been a collaboration from beginning to end. It presents an international group of ceramic artists who use the unglazed, naked surface to express their ideas and concerns. Through its definition, *Naked Clay* is able to cross a broad spectrum of processes, subject matter and context, from slipcasting to handbuilding, from figurative to conceptual, from domestic to public. My aim was to present not only the finished ceramics and techniques but also to investigate the ideas and areas of inspiration 'behind the scenes' in order to understand them further. This was accomplished by interviews and studio visits with 22 of the ceramicists presented – the rest of the material was gathered through correspondence. Nothing can beat a studio visit in order to achieve an intimacy and insight into work usually seen in the more detached context of a gallery or exhibition. To talk to the artist in their environment gives a profound appreciation of the 'why and how', enabling one to see the work holistically, to understand its essence, its beginnings and developments. This is what I hope to communicate to the reader.

Although each person presented here has a unique style and way of working, they are all connected through their committed relationship to their material. In his essay 'Craft and Art, Culture and Biology', Bruce Metcalf makes a comparison between the skill of an athlete or dancer and that of a craftsperson in the way bodily intelligence is manifested through exceptional motor control. The long apprenticeship to the material and its processes is underpinned by frustrations and disappointments which result in an 'unshakeable loyalty to the medium'. In other words, most of these ceramicists feel passionate about their work; not only through 'bodily intelligence' but also through the chameleon ability of clay to become a vehicle of expression for ideas and emotions. Thomas Hoadley describes his work as a collaboration between himself and the clay. Sara Radstone talks of the clay having the ability to do everything she needs. David Roberts says he is compelled to make pots and Gunhild Aaberg describes the powerful emotion of opening the kiln and feeling for her work as she feels for a man. I would say the ceramicist's relationship to clay is a kind of love affair.

It has been difficult to make a selection of work to be covered, and there were many ceramicists I wanted to include but was prevented from doing so through a practical lack of time and space. (I made a decision not to include woodfiring for instance partly because of these practicalities and the fact that flying ash can sometimes give a glaze-like surface.) The selection criteria I used were primarily work I could respond to, but also the desire to present a wide variety of styles from an international perspective. Working as a ceramicist can be a solitary, insular occupation and the research for this book has opened my eyes to many other ideas, philosophies and approaches to working with clay. Meeting the artists has been a privilege and an education.

Background

Naked Clay

As clothes are to the human body so are glazes to pots. That clay vessels made by primitive peoples were not glazed suggests a parallel to their own familiarity with nudity, nor does it seem inappropriate that they should have had the greatest feeling for naked clay forms. With our multiplicity of clothing we have become sophisticated and ashamed of our bodies, and, in a manner no less apposite have completely covered our pots with glazes.

BERNARD LEACH *A Potter's Book*

In the beginning there was no glaze. There was only clay. I first heard the expression 'naked clay' from the Swiss ceramicist Philippe Barde whose slipcast porcelain is presented here in the third chapter. Describing the qualities of unglazed ceramics, he said, 'With naked clay you can see the process – with glaze you will hide what is going on'. The ceramics selected for this book express specific qualities which would be lost through the glazing process. The dictionary defines naked as 'having no covering, bare, exposed; with no defence, protection or shield'. Many of the ceramicists here made a conscious decision to replace glazing with an investigation into some of the special qualities of naked clay. Their work represents a wide spectrum of styles and concerns.

The fundamental characteristic of unglazed clay is the quality of integration between form and surface rather than a separation between the elements of clay and glaze. Without the physical barrier of glaze, naked clay is able to invite an immediate response by revealing a range of direct aesthetic and tactile qualities. Glaze is basically glass and is hard, shiny, cold and when broken can cut. It is non-porous and reflects light. The unglazed surface gives the clay the possibility to breathe, feels softer and warmer to the touch and absorbs light. It can also take on the characteristics of other materials such as bone, wood, stone, marble, leather or velvet. The inspiration for unglazed ceramics can be drawn from many origins, and the artists presented in this book have developed their particular approaches from a number of culturally diverse sources.

Historical context of naked clay

Man and his imprint.
Man, who has no choice but to evolve.
Man, who noticed his own footprints in the
    clay.
Earth; vessels that contain life, vessels necess-
    ary for the survival of the family.
Forsaken in the cold and in the storm, prehis-
    toric human beings were forced
to use their intelligence to stay alive.
All of human evolution – art, science,
    commerce, politics – derives in a sense
from those earthen objects, formed and dec-
    orated by modelling.

BERNARD RUIZ-PICASSO, PICASSO'S GRANDSON.

The use of clay was developed independently by peoples living in different parts of the world, and was probably originally used in its raw state as a material for strengthening shelters or for tribal identification marks. From early times symbolic figures of men, women and animals were modelled in clay as part of the magic and religious rituals concerned with everyday life and fertility. Fragile

Pottery figure of reclining man made by the Chibcha peoples from the Columbian Andes during the first half of the 2nd millennium AD. Photograph courtesy of The Museum of Archaeology and Anthropology, Cambridge University.

pottery would not have been practical for nomadic peoples, and it was not until the New Stone Age that the making of pots started.

According to present knowledge, the earliest pottery, called Jomon ware, was made in 10,000BC in Japan. Early pottery was constructed by simple handbuilding techniques of coiling and paddling which required the minimum of tools. Decorative effects could be achieved by applying simple designs with coloured clays and pigments or scratching and impressing the clay surface to create a relief effect. Burnishing or polishing was widely used to give a smooth shiny appearance and partly seal

the porous surface. The work was fired without a kiln in the open, and sometimes carbonised or blackfired which could be controlled to give contrast of colour. Some time after 2000BC wheel and kiln technology (which led to glazing) spread from the Middle East through Europe, North Africa and the Far East, which in turn led to full-time production and growing professionalism. Over the next few millennia glaze technology gradually evolved and spread throughout Europe as a result of invasions and trade. However, the new technology was not synonymous in all civilisations at the same time and often paralleled older traditions, so that the two technologies ran side by

(Right) Raw pots waiting to be fired at Dawakin Tofa, a village in Kano state, Nigeria. Photograph by Joy Voisey.
(Below right) Votive horses and elephants from Gujarat, India. Photograph by Jane Perryman.

side. In the Americas for example, a rich tradition of unglazed pottery remained intact until the 16th century. There, potters were protected from invasion and the influence of new ceramic techniques until explorers and settlers arrived from Europe.

There are many traditional societies whose ceramics still remain unglazed in the 21st century; traditional potters from India, Africa, North and South America, Indonesia and Oceania as well as parts of the Middle and Near East, still work with low-temperature firing. Their technology has remained unchanged for millennia, representing unbroken traditions of pottery production. Some of the pottery remains from the Harappan civilisation (3000BC) on the Indus river for example, are similar in form, technique and decorative design to much of the pottery still being produced in northern India in the 21st century. In Gujarat today, sculpted terracotta horses are made for tribal worship, their forms having been repeatedly refined and honed since ancient times, so that the shape has been reduced to an abstract form and distilled to its very essence. In societies where cooking is carried out over an open fire and where there is no running water in the house, unglazed ware has practical advantages. Water can be kept cool by evaporation through the porous walls of low-fired earthenware and food can be cooked in a pot which will withstand the thermal shock of a direct flame – unlike higher-fired glazed pottery.

Contemporary influences on
naked clay

In Europe, the Industrial Revolution laid the foundations for the ceramics market we have today by producing a wealthy middle class who could afford to buy fine wares. Josiah Wedgwood was at the forefront of new innovations including two unglazed bodies called Black Basalt (a fine black porcelain) and Jasperware (an unglazed stoneware

resembling porcelain which could be coloured). The designs for these were inspired by classical Greek painted vases, an earlier form of unglazed ceramics. During the 20th century Bernard Leach combined the ideals of the Arts and Crafts Movement with his experience of living and studying in Japan. Studio Pottery as a movement took its lead from Leach, who began to train young potters during the 1920s in the production of utilitarian glazed pottery at his school in St Ives. Although glazing dominated his work, his use of restrained decorative surfaces and subtle glaze effects to achieve unity between form and surface have some connection with the qualities of unglazed ceramics.

William Staite Murray (who was a professor at the Royal College of Art) was a contemporary of Leach, but held very different views in that he promoted ceramics as art rather than craft. He successfully exhibited his own pots in galleries which usually only sold paintings. After the Second World War two émigrés arrived in Britain from Germany whose concerns were also very different to those of Leach. Lucie Rie and Hans Coper (an engineer by profession) shared an interest in contemporary architecture and design. They worked together at Rie's studio in London for ten years making tableware, and introduced the concerns of Modernism into ceramics: purity of concept, originality, principals of abstraction and a rejection of decoration. Their approach was urbane and their influence on the individually made ceramics produced today was highly significant. Coper's development of dry unglazed surfaces by rubbing oxides into the textured clay was innovative and contemporary, with qualities more in keeping with sculpture than with conventional ceramic traditions. Tony Birks says of him:

> He broke new ground with the shapes he made in fired clay, and in form, colour, surface and texture he created his own visual vocabulary. But it is not the outward manifestation of his technique alone which counts. If he influences others, it is in directing the modern potter towards a concept in pottery which is ancient in origin, but new in our time; fusing the functional with the cultural and symbolic.

In the 1960s Coper went on to teach at Camberwell School of Art, London and then at the Royal College of Art where he influenced generations of students. There is no 'Coper school' but his impact has been enormous, not only in his approach to the dry unglazed surface and refinement of form, but also in the way he changed our perception of ceramics. Edmund de Waal has said:

> Amongst Coper's and Rie's students are some of the foremost sculptural potters of today. Their influence is not so readily recognisable as that of Leach but is perhaps best seen in the valuing of work that has no ostensible utility and whose significance lies in more

abstract formal values. In looking and handling a pot and seeing and feeling it as a matrix of different sensations and proportions we may be seeing it not so much as a vessel for something but as a vessel that is something.

Another break with ceramic tradition came through the influence of 20th-century European and American painting. During the 1950s the freely painted ceramics of Picasso

(Opposite) *Stoneware Pot* by Hans Coper, height: 42 cm (16½ in.), 1968. Photograph courtesy of the Board of Trustees of the Victoria & Albert Picture Library.
(Above) *Vase-femme*, Vallauris, by Picasso, 47 x 17 cm (18½ x 6¾ in.). White fired clay, thrown, modelled and painted with engobe. Special collection. Photograph by Marc Domage © Images Modernes. © Succession Picasso/DACS 2004.

(some of which was painted with slips and left unglazed) became known and admired, and visual artists such as Leger, Miro and Chagall also worked with clay. These artists treated the ceramic surface as a canvas, painting directly and spontaneously rather than using a traditional decorating approach. New styles also began to develop in America at the same time which questioned the traditions of form and function. The American ceramicists were influenced by two major philosophies. The first was Zen Buddhism, which came from Japan and linked the act of making and firing with the Zen concepts of beauty – encouraging an interest in raku. The second was the ideas of the Abstract Expressionist artists. Peter Voulkos, a ceramicist from the west coast of America, was one of the forerunners of this approach and expressed his ideas through sculptural forms which challenged the craft-orientated traditions of functional pottery. Paul Soldner, a student of Voulkos, developed his own expressionist style, producing unglazed raku with oxides and stains.

By the 1960s ceramics in the west had become an accepted medium for self expression alongside painting and sculpture. Because of the unique ability of clay to mimic other materials many of the ceramic styles which followed echoed such art movements as Dadaism, Surrealism, Pop Art, Funk Art and Realism. As a result ceramic art gained considerable status in the gallery system. Unglazed ceramics were produced by such people as the Canadian Marilyn Levine who created super-realistic leather objects in high-fired stoneware complete with zippers and studs. She built up surface colour with slips which were stained and burnished to give an impression of *trompe l'oeil*. There were no longer any restraints; different methods of construction (throwing, slipcasting and handbuilding) were often combined in one piece. These diverse styles, imbued with multi-referencing and following no aesthetic boundaries, come under the umbrella of Postmodernism.

In Britain the Royal College of Art (whose role was originally to train young designers for the ceramics industry) has been dominant in developing new ideas in ceramics. From the 1970s, when David Queensbury took over the ceramics department, the demand for industrial designers was waning and the influence of studio pottery on the rise. He encouraged his students to explore traditional craft and technology and to find a place for

Cooling Towers Teapot (Variation no.36), by Richard Notkin, 17.5 x 23 x 9.5 cm (7 x 9 x 3¾ in.), 2001.

industrial techniques in the creative process. It was here that Jacqueline Poncelet experimented with the industrial material of bone china for her slipcast vessels and Glenys Barton used the same techniques and materials for her unglazed sculptural work in porcelain. More recently Felicity Aylieff adapted manufacturing and industrial techniques to develop an innovative clay body and mould-making technique for her sculpture. Many contemporary ceramicists working without glaze have been influenced either directly or indirectly by the Royal College's teaching and approaches. Elizabeth Fritsch, Jennifer Lee, Mo Jupp, Anna Noel, Lawson Oyekan, Felicity Aylieff and Nicholas Rena are all ex-graduates.

The rich unglazed ceramic traditions from Japan also represent an important source of influence for some of the ceramicists who work with naked clay. Neriage (where coloured clays are made into patterned blocks through

layering and compression), raku and black-firing are all techniques which express the importance of clay as material celebrated by the Japanese approach to ceramics.

Yixing ware from China is a style of unglazed utilitarian stoneware enjoying a long history of production and use dating back to the Sung Dynasty (960–1279). The production of Yixing teapots continues today and its tradition has influenced many contemporary ceramicists, both eastern and western. An example is the highly acclaimed American ceramicist Richard Notkin, who combines the influence of Yixing teapots with illusionism as a vehicle to express disturbing political images and messages.

Another approach to unglazed ceramics has developed via the influence of burnished low-fired pottery from traditional cultures. In the 1920s and 1930s the work of Native American Pueblo potters was being recognised and collected by museums in America. During the next few decades potters such as Maria Martinez and Lucy Lewis became 'stars', their work highly in demand by private collectors, galleries and museums. Books and articles were published about their work and processes which helped to inspire an interest in their traditional making, burnishing and firing techniques. In Britain during the early 1980s Magdalene Odundo from Kenya (also ex-Royal College) and Siddig el Nigoumi from the Sudan introduced handbuilding, burnishing and smoke-firing techniques from their native countries. Their work combined these traditions with a contemporary interpretation and inspired many ceramicists to explore 'low-tech' making and firing possibilities without the use of glaze.

The subject of this book is ceramics without glaze. In western society at the beginning of the 21st century unglazed ceramics perform very few utilitarian functions (terracotta plant pots and roof tiles come to mind as exceptions). Its purpose is as an art object. During the last two decades there has been a change of emphasis from functional studio pottery towards individual work. This kind of ceramic could be vessel or sculpturally based, but it fulfils the role of enriching daily life as an object of beauty and contemplation and a challenger of perceptions.

The value of work by deceased potters such as Hans Coper has wildly increased in the auction houses and given ceramics investment potential. In fact contemporary ceramics has been recognised by many collectors as an economical way to buy 'art'. However, the market for unglazed ceramics is not merely related to monetary value. In our society, dominated by sophisticated computerised technology and mass-produced consumer goods, there is a need for human beings to touch their roots and reconnect with some kind of spirituality. Some people achieve this by spending the day fishing beside water or flying a glider in the sky; for others the contemplation of a ceramic object whether in a domestic or public space can help to fulfil this need. After all, to carry on the metaphor of the elements, ceramic is basically the material of earth however disguised or sophisticated it is, and unglazed ceramics have a special elemental appeal. The Japanese ceramicist Yo Akiyama (who is presented in the first chapter) describes the power of ceramics to move us:

> When I am engaged in the processes of making and firing I am aware of the element of gravity. Earth draws everything towards itself. But I hope to touch heaven.

Further reading

Postmodern Ceramics, Mark Del Vecchio, Thames and Hudson, 2001

A Potter's Book, Bernard Leach, Faber and Faber, 1949

A History of World Pottery, Emmanuel Cooper, Batsford, 1988

Sculptural Ceramics, Ian Gregory, A&C Black, 1992

Women and Ceramics, Moira Vincentelli, Manchester University Press, 2000

Hans Coper, Tony Birks, Marston House, 1991

A Ceramic History, Edmund de Waal, Rufford Craft Centre website, www.ruffordcraftcentre.org.uk

Picasso Painter and Sculptor in Clay, ed. Marilyn McCully, Royal Acadamy of Arts, 1999

Traditional Pottery of India, Jane Perryman, A&C Black, 2000

Clay with Surface Pigment

Use of slips, oxides, stains on surface

The ceramicists in this section apply pigment directly onto the clay surface. They use a range of approaches and techniques to explore a variety of qualities such as light and shadow, pictorial composition, erosion, formal design and emotional expression. Wouter Dam repeatedly rubs oxides into the bisque surface of his sculptural forms and multi-fires to achieve a sense of depth through nuances of light and shadow. Elizabeth Fritsch also multi-fires, applying coloured slips and oxides to her vessels; integrating form and decoration through her concerns with *trompe l'oeil* and paradox. Sara Radstone achieves a restricted palette of grey colours through the application of oxides to the surface which is scratched and marked to express qualities of erosion. Anna Noel paints the bisque surface with oxides and slips to present timeless, mysterious qualities in her animal sculpture. Some of her work is raku fired with clay and glaze resists and fits more appropriately into the 'Clay Marked by Fire' chapter, but for the purposes of continuity I have included it here.

Elspeth Owen achieves a weathered, organic quality to her vessels by adopting an intuitive approach, direct painting with coloured slips onto the dry raw surface before burnishing. Nicholas Rena's sculptural work expresses contradicting emotional qualities of both detachment and tactile sensuality. He uses an unorthodox method of building up depth of colour through multi-applications of coloured inks which are absorbed into the porous bisque surface before sanding and bleaching back. Ray Meeker is able to present his passionate political beliefs concerning the environment through an expressive approach, painting slips and oxides onto the surfaces of sculptural pieces.

(Opposite) *Upright Being,* by Gunhild Aaberg ht: 22 cm (8¾ in.), 1997.

Wouter Dam

Wouter Dam in his studio.

Photograph by Jane Perryman.

(Opposite) *Red Sculpture,* 23 x 22 x 23 cm
(9 x 8¾ x 9 in.), 2001.

Photograph by R. Scobye.

Wouter Dam's Amsterdam studio is above the canal which leads to Harlaam; while working he can glance down at traditional Dutch sailing vessels with their round bows and voluptuous curves and think about sailing through Holland on his own boat. It is easy to interpret the scene as a metaphor for his minimalist abstract sculpture which, like a boat, is horizontally orientated. Without the support of water as a leveller, it takes on a new identity of its own. Just as a boat moves through water, travelling through space and time, Dam's sculpture invites us to move through it, expressing a sense of coming and going. We are left with the kind of rich associations experienced on a journey.

Dam describes the essence of his work:

The pieces of sculpture I create exhibit traces of very different things, such as the shapes of classical vases due to their beautifully balanced shapes; Neolithic or Iron Age pots with their very warm, intimate and human feel to the shape; and body parts with their sensuous shapes and curves emphasised by the velvet-like surfaces that I apply to my pieces. A single piece can evoke both the coldness of the parts of a machine and at the same time a sensuality reminiscent of the human shape.

Other sources for my work are shapes found in nature, such as fruits, the buds of flowers, and the shells of sea creatures. The shapes of boats are also used, something I am able to observe when sailing throughout Holland on my own boat. Although these things are no doubt sources of inspiration, one thing is very important to me; they should just be a vague memory of the real thing, just a hint. There should be enough room for the viewer to let his own imagination run free.

Over the years it has become more and more clear that the most important aspect of my work is the contrast between round and flat surfaces when the two meet at sharp angles, thereby interrupting the soft curving surfaces with abrupt lines. Another important aspect is the openness of the piece. My

(Above) *Blue Shape,* 26 x 23 cm (10¼ x 9 in.), 2001.
Photograph by R. Scobye.

(Opposite) *Yellow Sculpture,* 23 x 28 x 25 cm
(9 x 11 x 9¾ in.), 2001.
Photograph by R. Scobye.

latest work, for example, is open on both sides to reveal even more of the inside. Although today my work is fully sculptural and completely removed from being a functional object, it still bears some resemblance to its original form.

Early life as the child of an architect who collected contemporary ceramics of the 1960s equipped Dam with visual orientation and a familiarity with volume and space. He says he needs only to walk around a building once to know where he is – he can 'turn the space around in his head'. At the Rietveldt Academy in Amsterdam he studied ceramics under Jan van der Vaart and developed a passion for the wheel, spending three months in a small traditional factory throwing flower pots. His early work was design orientated through affordable limited editions of slipcast functional ware. Over a period of ten years the symmetry and repetition became tedious and the initial step of removing glaze from the rims of bowls in order to create a focal point became the catalyst for change. He started to turn the bowl and vase forms on their side and the metamorphosis from functional to non-functional

was immediate. He realised the limitation of the upright form was over; he had transformed the vase into another dimension.

In the late 1980s my pieces became more asymmetrical, so much so that they tended to fall over to one side. This was corrected by adding a clay ring to one side of the bottom of the piece, then doing away with the bottom ring altogether, thereby letting the piece become a reclining object. By merely laying it on its side, I was able to let the shape waver out into many directions without the fear of the vessel falling over. This was a significant moment as it allowed me to play freely with the vessel while shaping it, and to treat the inside as importantly as the outside.

Realising non-functional pieces do not require glaze and observing how glaze blurs the edges of form, he tentatively began to remove the glaze, gradually taking one strip away at a time until it was abandoned completely. He began to experiment with the application of oxide in-between firings to build up depth and richness. Recognition for his work came through a substantial state grant in 1992, encouraging him to pursue this new direction. Early on in his career Dam had made a deliberate decision to avoid teaching as a way to financial support, believing it would stifle his progression as an artist. The last ten years had been a struggle living on state benefit and taking construction jobs to support his income, so this financial cushion was very helpful in the evolution of his new ideas. His work could now progress without the interruption of odd-jobbing.

Making sequence
(Top left) Thrown rings.
(Top right) The rings have been joined together
and a section removed.
(Above left) A slab of clay is folded; the profile
marked out and cut.
(Above right) The folded sections are manoeuvred, spliced
into the main piece and joined.

He continues to describe the next stage of development:

Opening the shapes more and more, even adding contrasting lines that run all the way around and into the vessel, leads your eye specifically into and back out of the shape. Another way of achieving this is by the use of contrast between a light colour on the inside and a dark one on the outside, or the other way around. After exploring the many possibilities of this concept, I started to feel its limitations and the need for an even more drastic step towards opening the vessel completely on both sides, thereby revealing everything and abandoning any sense of direction to the vessel. Working in this way for almost four years now, I still do not see an end to all the possibilities, although I am aware that the next step would be to cut open the tube-like shape.

The whole development could only take place because I have always made objects purely as decorative pieces. One could look at it as a movement from the most completely enclosed inside space of a vessel, designed to keep things well concealed, to vases and bowls that hold things but also partly reveal or even present them to the outside world, to a complete opening up of the inside so that there are no secrets, no concealment, and everything can move freely throughout the vessel, almost as if the spirit, hidden inside the vessel, can finally move freely in and around it.

Dam uses a combination of throwing and slabbing techniques to construct his pieces. He starts by throwing 7–8 rings on the wheel and rolling out some flat clay slabs; the limitation of these shapes give him a framework and definition for the possibilities of assemblage and form. The rings are kept wet so that the clay remains soft enough to manoeuvre after the distortion caused by cutting. The slabs are folded and literally spliced into the main form which will finally be made from 2–4 of the thrown sections. During the assemblage Dam will have a certain form in mind which is based on a development from the last batch, but it is the combination of inspiration and intuition that guides him to the final solution. With each new group of work he always adds an 'experiment piece' which will possibly lead to something new.

When leatherhard the pieces are scraped until smooth, then sanded to give them a direction of marks. This attention to finish gives the work a taut and bulbous quality as if the space inside is about to burst out. After the initial bisque firing of 1050°C (1922°F) the colour is achieved by rubbing oxides and body stains into the bisque with his fingers before refiring to 1200°C (2192°F). This is repeated between two and four times to give depth, resulting in a velvety, seductive surface – Dam draws the analogy to a Rothko painting. His palette is limited to dark black/brown to red, yellow, green and intense blue or sometimes the off-white colour of the fired clay. Most pieces are treated to one colour enabling shadow to play an important role in defining the form and emphasising his exploration of inside/outside. The rims surrounding the apertures are often left without pigment to further accentuate the form. Occasionally he uses a thin line of contrasting colour to circumnavigate the centre of the form leading the eye in continuous motion from inside to outside.

Dam says that he aims to make pieces whose perfect balance results in an interesting view from every angle; logical yet not predictable. To see his work in the flesh is to be struck by his mastery of both enclosing space and allowing space to move within clay walls, almost like a ceramic architect. David Pagel, reviewer for the *Los Angeles Times* has described his work as 'Table Top Sculpture'. The dimension of Dam's work (up to 37 cm/ 14½ in. long) is limited by technique and kiln size, but one could easily imagine a transition in scale from domestic to public sculpture.

Further reading

'International Exhibitions – Wouter Dam', Shane Enright, *Crafts* magazine, May 1999

In/Outside Ceramic Millennium, 1999, Amsterdam catalogue

'In/Outside' Thomas Piche Jnr, *Ceramic Review* no. 187

Elizabeth Fritsch

Listening to an interview with Elizabeth Fritsch for Radio 3's programme *Private Passions* (Easter 2001) gave a fascinating insight into the way music has informed and inspired her work. The opportunity to select and discuss favourite pieces of music in the context of her life and ceramics was particularly illuminated by her choice of Bach's Preludes nos 5 and 10 from *The Well-Tempered Clavier*. In this piece the rhythm is flowing and unified, underpinned by the precision of technique and counterpoint – yet it also retains the quality of stillness. The vocabulary used to describe music can also apply to

(Above) *Water of Greenness,* ht: (approx.) 44 cm (17¼ in.), 1990.
Photograph by Alexander Brattell.
(Right) *Ghost Trio,* max. ht: 55.5 cm (21¾ in.), 1993–5.
Photograph by Alexander Brattell.

(Opposite) *Blown Away – Green Horn Vase with Turbulent Vase,* ht: 46 cm (18 in.). Photograph by Alexander Brattell.

the visual arts, and when used in the context of Fritsch's work, is especially relevant. She has said:

> The geometric tonal structures and rhythm figures in music have a flowing dynamic vitality – a kind of levity, which corresponds with my rhythmic and geometric aspirations of painted colour on form.

Other references such as Flemish primitive painting, Renaissance fresco painting, world literature, archaeology, geology and quantum physics are also evident in her work. She talks of her eclecticism as important 'feeding' periods in between exhibitions where the stimulation of studying, reading, reflecting, of going to exhibitions and concerts can later fuel her productive making periods.

It is significant that Fritsch has chosen the vessel as her form because of its familiar references to intimacy and domestic life. To see the forms in their naked pre-painted stage is to see them in this comfortable state. Through the painting a dramatic transformation takes place, launching them completely into another dimension. This is what Fritsch calls two and a half dimensions; on one hand the piece is obviously solid and rounded, but at the same time its surface painting indicates the tricks and *trompe l'oeil* of pictorial perspective. She also talks of the fourth dimension where part of a painted box or triangular shape overlaps another so that both can be read independently. Logically we know the part that overlaps cannot exist. One thinks of an Escher painting.

Another theme is the fault lines running through the design where it shifts and drops or lifts, linking to rhythm and tempo shifts in music or the fault lines in rock strata. All her work is metaphorical and paradoxical so that what we see is not only an actual pot but also the representation of a pot, closely related to the kind of representation we would see in a still-life painting. Fritsch discovered fairly early in her career that by grouping several related vessels together she could emphasise a dialogue through the dynamic of their relationship to each other. Recently she has been working in monochrome with forms inspired by architecture and water such as leaning towers, ziggurats, boat forms and waves.

Fritsch grew up on the Welsh borders, her visual orientation for man-made art focused on the Gothic cathedral at Chester where she spent many hours absorbing its soaring interior spaces. The design at Ironbridge also fascinated her and she has since remarked that such exquisitely poised precision engineering and industrial landscape can be as inspiring as sculpture. Trained as a harpist, she studied music at the Birmingham School of Music and then at the Royal Academy, but after graduation chose not to follow the expected musical career. She talks about the regret and guilt felt by abandoning her music lessons, but later came to realise that her love and knowledge of music was able to feed her visual work.

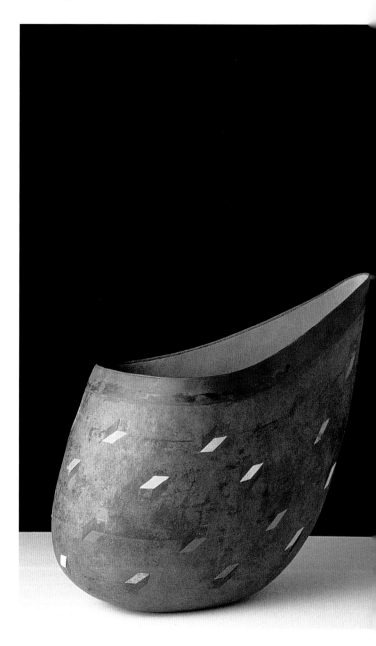

Green Horn Vase, ht: 35 cm (13¾ in.), 1994.

Photograph by Alexander Brattell.

I was not cut out to be a performer – I'm an ideas person and like to work alone in the studio – composing would have been more suitable. I needed some manual labour.

Like many ceramic artists she found pottery by chance. When pregnant with her first child a friend gave her some clay which she 'messed around with' on the kitchen table. Finding she was attracted to its elemental qualities she carried on experimenting for a couple of years before applying to the Royal College of Art (partly because she'd heard there were crèche facilities). Handbuilding is compatible with the practicalities of early child rearing. Fritsch discovered an empathy with the material and enjoyed the contemplative effects of repetition building with strips of clay. This quality of peacefulness experienced at the making stage emerges intact in the finished work and gives it a quality of classical tranquillity, like a Piero della Francesca painting. At the RCA she was taught by Hans Coper who encouraged her to explore the painted surface and find her own voice. She remembers him as a wonderful teacher who adapted his teaching to the student's needs rather than imposing his ideas upon them. She was never keen to explore the alchemy of glazing or the practicalities of tableware, preferring the dry matt surface and taking her form beyond the functions of use. She made extensive investigations into coloured slips, applying them to the surface within a framework. By using the grid as a time signature she was able to make the design fit the form. Coper had taught her the importance of total integration between the decoration and the form of the pot, and it is this quality which gives her work its unique distinction and power

Her first solo show in 1974 at the Waterloo Place Gallery in London established her as a major new voice on the British craft scene. Despite national and international recognition she talks about the 1970s as a period of economic hardship, of 'living on the breadline'. Ironically, the decision to have a second child was the catalyst for improving the value of her work and so her standard of living. From past experience of her first-born she anticipated the ease of combining ceramics with having a baby, but her daughter proved to be much more extrovert and required full-time attention. Fritsch was unable to work for three years and as demand exceeded supply, the prices

Tornado Trio, ht: (approx.) 59 cm (23¾ in.), 2000.
Photograph by Alexander Bratte.

shot up in the auction houses. Since the mid-1980s her work has enjoyed a rarefied, elevated status with collectors and museums. Upon hearing a piece was up for sale at an auction in New York the curator from a Japanese museum was keen to add it to the museum's collection of four. He flew halfway around the world in order to secure it.

The pieces are handbuilt, using flattened coils or ribbons of clay joined together by pinching slowly to create the form. The clay is a 50/50 mixture of smooth and grogged (T-Material or C-Material) stoneware bodies fired to 1260°C (2300°F). The surface is handpainted with coloured slips, oxides and underglaze colours involving three to six different firings (1200°C–1260°C/2192°F–2300°F). Fritsch does not make preliminary drawings but works directly and intuitively. She talks of improvisation in the same way that a jazz musician practises his art form. She deliberately works with the radio or television playing to stop herself thinking

Time Trio, ht: 25 cm (9¾ in.), 2000. Photograph by Alexander Brattell.

and encourage her intuitive side to dominate. She allows the work to go in its own direction.

Here Fritsch talks of the three main elements of her work (from *Vessels from Another World* by Edward Lucie-Smith):

The primary preoccupation is with the way the three aspects of colour, form and rhythm can be made to activate and emphasise each other (as they do in music).

1. Colour
The aim is for the clarity, precision and spatial depth of ancient fresco. The whites and celestial blues of

the 1970s and 1980s have given way temporarily to more glowing 'twilight' and shadowy colours with increasing use of counterpoint, overpainting and layered impasto. The coloured slips are always applied with brushes, giving an unevenness. The layering of colours produces unpredictable tonal variations, occasionally semi-transparencies, and shadows, together with much breaking through from one colour to another.

2. Form
The aim here is form following 'otherworldly' function. So the forms tend to be surreal, gestural (often leaning forward or pointing upwards, as for example

Trio of Spout Pots, ht: 59 cm (23¼ in.), 2000.
Photograph by Alexander Brattell.

in many of the 'blown away' funerary vases), and in many different ways metaphorical (e.g. Quantum Pockets, River and Moon pots, Shadow Vessels, Spiral Vases, collisions of particles in curved space, lachrymatories, parent and child groups, mountain pots, mythical images, etc.). Another main preoccupation is with the placing of the forms in assemblages and clusters so that they energise each other.

3. Rhythm
The painted rhythm figures are not intended to be decorative, but to be both intrinsic to the form (as is rhythm in music and dance) and intrinsic to the colour, carrying clusters of colour in a variety of ways, e.g. cross-rhythms, counterpoint, particle collisions, etc. Rhythms are always derived from the form, and so are essentially modified by that form (i.e. not 'stuck on'). Paradoxically, the more speedy the rhythm, the longer it takes to paint; but the capacity to spend endless hours painting one piece of work is the result of a nonchalance towards linear time and not particularly 'painstaking'. A certain precision, however, is of the essence in expressing rhythm.

Notes on Pots about Equilibrium, 1993
There is an emphasis on equilibrium in the form between the opposing forces of left to right, front and back, inside and outside, two and three dimensions, weightiness and lightness, etc., producing in a normal vase or vessel a mood of abnormal suspense and elation.

When it comes to the painted surface, the use of colour and rhythm figures to emphasise the form (as in music) involves balancing opposing forces of more paradoxical and almost metaphysical nature; the various fragmentations and counterpoint between light and dark, sharp and soft, upper and lower layers, rhythmic clusterings, etc. This whole two- and three-dimensional interplay in curved space might seem impossibly busy and chaotic, but when married faithfully to a given form can be peaceful, even timeless.

At a recent symposium in Switzerland we both attended, Elizabeth Fritsch passed one of her pieces around for inspection. It was a tall slim lachrymatory – surprisingly light and vulnerable to the touch. The processes of making were evident; the flat coiling lines faintly discernible and the qualities of handpainting embraced rather than disguised. It felt strangely poignant to be holding something which is mainly experienced behind glass or through photography. In Japan leading practitioners of traditional crafts can earn the status of 'Living Cultural Treasure'. Edward Lucie-Smith has suggested that Fritsch would qualify as our candidate in the United Kingdom. I would have to agree.

Further reading
Elizabeth Fritsch, Vessels from Another World: Metaphysical Pots in Painted Stoneware, Edward Lucie-Smith, Bellew Publishing Company Ltd. in collaboration with the Northern Centre for Contemporary Art, 1993
'Elizabeth Fritsch – Metaphysical Vessels' by Jane Hamlyn, *Ceramic Review,* no. 148

Anna Noel

The romance of Anna Noel's working and living environment is a fitting backdrop for the creation of her dreamlike, ethereal animal sculptures. Since the mid-80s she has been based at her family home, a Welsh long farmhouse with views over the sea at Brandy Cove on the Gower peninsula near Swansea. The area is littered with Neolithic remains and rich with legends and folklore concerning shipwrecks and smuggling. A tunnel still connects the beach to the farmhouse kitchen and it is said the cries of manacled press gangs, left to drown in a shipwreck, can still be heard at night. Noel's primary relationship to the world is through animals. She is in constant contact with domestic animals, farm animals and wild ponies which live amongst a surrounding landscape of rocky cliffs and heathland, providing her with subject matter and inspiration.

> If I'm quiet I can approach an animal slowly and go right up to them. Then they feel safe with you. When you are with an animal you have this great moment with them – you are with a different species. When you see a horse and rider silhouetted against the skyline it's a powerful and magical image; an archetypal figure in folklore. It transcends time; it is timeless . . . it has a special quality . . . it is mysterious – where is it going? Where has it come from? The image taps into journeys. There are lots of riders here plus wild ponies on the commons and beaches of the Gower. You never know when they'll turn up. On the north of the Gower there are little bits of higher ground in the salt marshes next to the sea; with the mist it looks as if the horse is rising up out of the water.

Noel's sculptures capture that moment of stillness but intense alertness when an animal is first aware of a human being – all its attention focused on 'flight or fight' – whether to escape intrusion into its world or stand its ground. Her work holds a specific quality of stillness but is by no means static; her animals contain an energy which could be unleashed at any moment. Noel has chosen the horse, a universally recognised symbol of

Portrait of Anna Noel.
Photograph by Jane Perryman.

(Opposite) *Horse and Riders,* ht: 40 cm (15¾ in.).

Goat, ht: 23 cm (9 in.). Photograph by Graham Matthews.

Horse and Rider, ht: 40 cm (15¾ in.). Photograph by Graham Matthews.

power and mystery from ancient mythology to modern times, as a dominant theme. Her horses sometimes stand alone looking into the distance and sometimes support bareback riders. Noel's horses are light and carefree, strangely disassociated from the world and from their riders, yet the two seem to belong together in a symbiotic partnership. Apart from farm animals (goats, pigs and cows) another favourite theme is her exploration of dogs, particularly the greyhound whose form is elegant and streamlined, bred for speed. Associated with Welsh mythology and linked to the underworld, the greyhound's role was to accompany the mythical character and

provides Noel with another connection between the animal and human figure.

Noel grew up in an environment where the art and craft of making things was part of life; her father an architect, her mother an art teacher. An early experience at fourteen years old of handmodelling with self-hardening clay was addictive, and led to studying figurative sculpture at school followed by a degree at Bath Academy. Here she was inspired by various visiting lecturers overseen by John Colbeck and began to explore the themes of circus and fairground imagery, linking together her interest in folk art and children's stories. Although gallery response was positive to her early work, she found her press-moulding technique became restrictive and lifeless.

A postgraduate course at the Royal College of Art encouraged a change in making technique in order to develop her forms and find new levels of expression. Press-moulding was replaced by wrapping and rolling slabs of clay to form the bodies and limbs of her animals, giving a new spontaneity to her work and freeing her to work towards a larger scale. It was also at the Royal College that she abandoned glaze and developed the dry surface with oxides and slips that she continues to use today. Access to London museums and galleries equipped her with an eclectic personal vocabulary, with allusions to Marini Marino, Chagall, English Staffordshire figurines and Toby jugs. She began to investigate the use of narrative as a way to connect animals and humans through the surreal humour of Edward Lear limericks.

The forms are simplified and stylised with minimal detail and clarity of line which enables the eye to move from one part to another with ease. They express an effortlessness in their metamorphosis from clay objects to the animal kingdom. Pieces are made from a 50/50 mix of T-Material and white stoneware and built slowly with soft slabs of clay, starting with the legs and constructing up through body, neck and head. By working with soft clay Noel is able to manipulate the form by folding and pushing the various components of the body while keeping possibilities flexible and open to improvisation. After joining, the clay is beaten with a wooden stick and pushed out from the inside with fingers and tools to shape it and give it volume. A horse or animal with four standing legs is built and fired on a support to avoid collapse, and this is carried through to the bisque firing to avoid distortion.

Greyhound, ht: 23 cm (9 in.).

Pieces are covered with a thin porcelain slip before bisque firing to 1020°C (1868°F); some are then treated with oxides and coloured slips before refiring to 1100°C (2012°F). By using copper and cobalt in different strengths she is able to achieve a range of blues and greens which together with whites through greys, browns and blacks provide her limited palette. Other pieces are treated with a resist raku technique resulting in a distinctive animal skin marking. The bisque is covered first with a resist slip and then a raku glaze. During the raku firing the glaze begins to melt, is withdrawn and covered with sawdust so that during cooling some parts are exposed to encourage lighter areas. After the firing the outer layer of glaze will fall away to reveal smoke marking due to cracking and crazing of the glaze and slip.

Making sequence – (Above) Different body parts are built with soft slabs which are folded and moulded into shape.

(Opposite above) The different parts have been joined together, then beaten into shape with a stick.
(Opposite below) After bisque the surfaces are treated with oxides and slips before re-firing.
Photographs by Jane Perryman.

Further Reading

'Looking Afresh', Josie Walter, *Ceramic Review* no. 185

Sara Radstone

(Above) Sara Radstone in her studio.

(Opposite) *Triptych*, ht: 168 cm (66¼ in.), 1998.

Photograph by Philip Sayer.

A few weeks after seeing Sara Radstone's exhibition at the Barrett Marsden Gallery in London I was driving on a country road at night across the rolling hills of the Suffolk/Cambridgeshire border. It was full moon and for a few moments I turned off the headlights to enjoy the moonlight illuminating the road and surrounding bleak wintry landscape of open fields. The ribbon of road stretched ahead, its parallel lines converging to a point in the distance. Moonlight reflected on its surface and produced many shades of silvers, greys, and grey blues which changed constantly as the car travelled forward. An acute awareness of the interplay between space, time and light transported me back to her work in the gallery and gave an increased insight into what it is about.

For over 20 years Radstone has been producing ceramic sculpture which explores the erosion of form and surface over time. The dictionary defines the word erode as 'to gnaw away, destroy gradually, wear out'. This can apply to the material world of natural and man-made objects as well as the spiritual world of atmosphere, emotions and memory. The raw emotion of bereavement for example, erodes over time as the pain and loss transforms into a dull ache and then becomes a distant memory. There have been references in her work to the kind of urban obsolescence we see every day on the streets, such as discarded crumpled paper and metal drink cans, or of the layers of torn paper on advertisement hoardings. Allusion to rock forms and the erosion of its surface by weather and time is also there, but not in any kind of literal way. Radstone's work is essentially elusive rather than a concrete interpretation and leaves us with a strong sense of association and atmosphere. It contains the contradiction of somehow being both present and absent at the same time.

Radstone grew up in an atmosphere which encouraged an early interest in art. Her father was a dealer in 18th- and 19th-century paintings and her mother a 'bohemian' bookseller who was involved in the arts and introduced her daughter to the art world through exhibitions and galleries. She started Saturday morning pottery classes at the age of four years and from this early experience of clay knew she wanted to be a potter or sculptor.

Living in London meant she was able to visit the British and Victoria & Albert Museums regularly where she was instantly attracted towards the collections of ancient pots. A love and empathy for clay was in place from the beginning.

The foundation course at Hereford College of Art and Design was followed by a degree at Camberwell College of Art in London from 1976–79. At the time sculptural ceramics was being encouraged at Camberwell in order to break away from the traditions of studio pottery. Scott Chamberlain came over from the US on a fellowship to work with the students, bringing fresh ideas of breaking down boundaries between art and craft. He encouraged Radstone to 'follow her heart'. Supported by Ewen Henderson her tutor, she looked for a way to combine the qualities of ancient artefacts with the detritus of sophisticated urban life, expressing her ideas through coiled vessels. She talks about the connections between the thumb prints which remain visible and intact on ancient pots and the thumb print of modern humanity on discarded objects.

After college she was immediately offered a solo exhibition and joined 401½ studios, working closely with Angus Suttie. She started her career by making non-functional handbuilt vessels, describing them as 'vessels about pots'. Gradually she developed an interest in exploring

(Above) Detail from *Triptych*.

(Opposite) *Untitled*, w: 70 cm (27½ in.), 1998.

Photograph by Philip Sayer.

the surface like a three-dimensional canvas with slips, oxides, scratches and marking. Finding her use of colour was obscuring the form and interior space of her work she began developing an elemental palette of greys which could absorb and reflect light. Radstone has said, 'What I love about clay is the use of light which describes the form – it does the work for the piece'. She investigated ways to find new shapes and discovered slabbing as a technique to push her work into a new dimension. After five years she set up Arlington studios in Brixton with three other ceramicists and combined studio work with teaching at various art schools.

The new space at Arlington was a significant motivating force in Radstone's development and her work changed, becoming more sculptural and increasing in scale. The forms became enclosed with a single opening cut across their top surface, and instead of springing upwards started to lie down so that they appeared more informal. Because of concern over an opening in the ceramic form Radstone found herself in a paradoxical situation. After making an enclosed piece she would chip out a hole when nearly dry, so that association to the form as a vessel could remain securely in place. Whenever she showed slides of her work she was asked 'Where is the opening?', a question with no relevance had she worked with another material such as stone or bronze. A sculptor

friend gave her Gaston Bachelard's book *The Poetics of Space* which became a catalyst for further change. The sentence which particularly captivated her was 'there is always more in a closed than an open box'. Complete closure of the forms led Radstone into the exploration of interior space, of showing work in pairs and groups and then ultimately into the use of installation.

Now Radstone's studio is in the garden at her London home and it is remarkable to see how such a small working environment can produce work of such significance. Over the years she has worked with dry slabs of clay, pinching and building up the shape instinctively – the dry surface retaining its history of making, revealing fingermarks, careful seams and scratches. This intuitive approach evolved through a desire to make work through recognition rather than decision, and sometimes the forms which emerged would surprise her. Working on several pieces at once, she cut up discarded pieces into sections and re-arranged them to make new forms in a process of construction. Recently she has been using sketches and planning her work so that her groups and installations fit the exhibition space. After bisque firing the surfaces are covered with an off-white vitreous slip, then painted with a wash of black stain which is rubbed back to reveal surface unevenness. Further scratched marks or inscriptions are then made before firing to cone 7.

Scratching incisions through the rubbed black stain and slip before re-firing.

Alison Britton talks of Radstone as:

making objects that increasingly resist classification and ceramic prediction – stretched lines, like fencing poles, waterspouts, the handle of a hoe, long limbs, hollow reeds. They are elongating far beyond the size of her kiln, and are recomposed of segments, beautifully joined with plastic metal. They are not obvious; they are lying, leaning, hanging, like shadows lurking in corners, blips in the line of vision.

It has been a long slow process of simplifying, stripping down, abstracting, from vessels to sack shapes to horizontal boxes, forms that lean, and 'Little Volumes' lined up on the wall. Pots normally stand up, and we are used to the anthropomorphism of the upright, evident container. Radstone's pots gradually closed up their apertures to slits and some of the pieces reclined like angular chests or cubist limbs.

A recent installation of 44 wall-mounted books continued her theme of volume and contained space. They presented us with a double meaning of both the book and the spaces between the pages which hold a record of the containment of memories. By firing the 'books' the memories are made permanent into a kind of memorial to the death of a loved one; the pages covered with indiscernible messages and texts. Over the years Radstone has developed a level of skill where she can control the many processes of ceramics in order to express unique qualities of atmosphere and emotion. She has said:

The clay has done everything I want – I can make it do what I need.

(Left) *Corpus* (detail).
Photograph by Philip Sayer.

(Bottom) *Corpus,* each piece 20 x 30 x 4 cm (8 x 11¾ x 1½ in.),
2002. Photograph by Philip Sayer.

Further reading

'Hard Lines', Alison Britton, catalogue by Barrett Marsden
    Gallery, November 1998
'The Consolations of Time and Place: New Work by Sara
    Radstone', Linda Sandino, catalogue by Barrett
    Marsden Gallery, February 2002
'Sara Radstone at Barrett Marsden Gallery', Oliver
    Watson, *Ceramic Review,* no. 195
'Sara Radstone', Angus Suttie, *Ceramic Review,* no. 100

Elspeth Owen

Elspeth Owen in her studio.

Photograph by Jane Perryman.

Elspeth Owen's studio is a wooden cricket pavilion overlooking Grantchester meadows in Cambridge. It is a secret place hidden from the road by dense conifers and surrounded by a thick hedge. It is very much her territory. Owen's work and its place of creation are inextricably linked; nothing has changed for as long as I can remember going there and it is unimaginable to think of her making pots anywhere else. She works sitting on a chair facing the light, surrounded by natural forms such as pebbles, driftwood, shells and dried plants. Three shelves and a wooden table are covered with her work. The pots are shaped with her hands and fingers, cradled and cushioned tenderly like a baby in her lap. There is a timeless quality here tinged with fragility and vulnerability and the paradox of permanence/impermanence. Attached to the wall is a photocopy of the Zen quote:

> Is it possible to remember being born? My Zen master never tires of saying that it is impossible for anyone to remember being born, and likewise that it is impossible to know that one is dead. This is, in simple terms, the basis for the Zen teaching that there is neither birth nor death, and underlines the importance of realising who it is that thinks it was born and thinks it will die.
>
> DAGAKU RUMME, FUKUI, JAPAN

Owen's commitment to life as a potter, which she refers to as a romantic occupation, has sustained and supported her for over 20 years. Although she also works as an artist with installations, photography and video, making pots represents the major part of her work. She says:

> Pots are the most fundamental image of civilisation with a range of functions from containing salt to human remains. The most important thing about pots is that they are old but new – we are renewing all the time.

She sees a parallel between her way of working with that of the Inuit sculptors of the Arctic, who believe that when they carve a figure it is merely being released from a place where it

(Below) *Bowl,* w: 36 cm (14¼ in.), 1999.

Photograph by James Austin.

(Bottom) *Pillow,* dia: 28 cm (11 in.), 2000.

Photograph by James Austin.

exists already. This idea is prevalent amongst other pre-industrialised cultures where, like Owen, the artist has a strong spiritual connection with his material and environment. The Native American Pueblo potters believe their clay and burnishing stones to be sacred; the Asian Indian potters believe that in working with the sacred elements of earth, fire and water they are creating objects imbued with the spirit of god.

Owen's training as an academic and later psychotherapist cultivated her skills as a wordsmith. Like many others whose careers later turned to ceramics she was introduced to clay by attending evening classes in order to 'miss bath-time with the kids' – in other words, as a night off from family life. She remembers finding the precision of glazing intimidating, of trying to overcome such problems as glaze crawling and overfiring; the frustration of glaze sticking to kiln shelves. Within two years she acquired her own kiln and set up a studio in the garden house. Her first experiments revolved

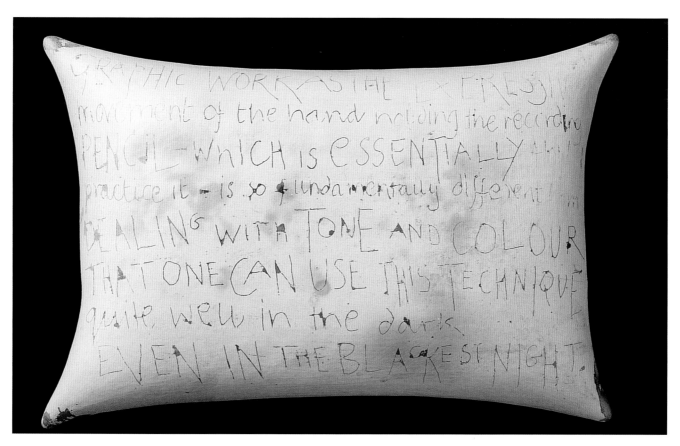

Jar, ht: 36 cm (14¼ in.), 2002. Photograph by Graham Murrell.

around adding colour directly to the clay to achieve a rougher, more battered look.

> It felt like cheating; there's a bit of me that wants to break rules or get away with something.

In 1975 the opportunity to lease the cricket pavilion at Grantchester from King's College, Cambridge provided Owen with a conducive environment and plenty of space to begin investigating her ideas. Significantly, the new studio remained empty for a year while she travelled in New Guinea, but this incubation period enabled her to make the mental shift to become a potter.

For someone who was primarily self-taught, she was fortunate to meet and impress Henri Rothschild, who exhibited and introduced her work nationally. This early success, supported by an article in *Crafts* magazine written by Martina Margetts, encouraged her to keep working; the repetition of forming pots by hand bringing its own gradual development. In the early 1990s Owen began to explore other media such as photography, video and installation which included clay objects to express her political ideas and major emotional experiences. An activist in the Women's Movement, particularly the Greenham Common peace protests of the 1980s, had led to a photographic and video installation *The Way Women Walk.*

Later, work completed at a residency in Banff, Canada helped to consolidate her response to the death of her mother. She made 85 small clay spheres representing her mother's age which were floated on milk inside a wooden coffin supported on wheels. Over the next few years she exhibited several more installations on this theme including *Dry Tears* where her mother's handkerchiefs were dipped in clay slip and fired; the paradox of their cremation and survival alluding to the memory of a loved one after death. There is a permanent installation in her studio: *Tree House*, a simplified house form constructed from chestnut logs cut for firewood with a pure white polished porcelain sphere in the middle. In August 1993 an enormous chestnut tree had fallen onto the pavilion, shaking the building and breaking many pots inside the studio. The installation explores the idea of fragility in a permanent house, emphasised by the contrast of the smooth white clay with the rough wood.

It is difficult to look at Owen's pots without experiencing a powerful urge to pick them up. It is the combination of a strong tactile message through the smooth or cracked surfaces with a curiosity/anticipation of their weight. The walls are delicate but at the same time the piece feels substantially well grounded because of the thicker base. For

Tree House, 1994, ht: 3.5m (11 ft), chestnut and pinched porcelain. Photograph by Nicolette Hartlett.

many years her forms evolved from the natural action of pinching, a rounded bottom curving into a slight flaring out and coming in, usually with a defining rim or neck. A very female form. Over time the forms have become clearer and more refined, developing into open bowls, straight-sided more vertically orientated forms and spheres. Some pieces are made from slabs such as the clay 'pillows' with four well-defined corners covered with the poetry of Paul Klee.

For 25 years Owen's basic forming method has remained the same. She works with a smooth or textured white Earthstone clay, forming the clay into a sphere then supporting it with her right hand while pinching out the shape with her thumb and left middle finger, sometimes turning it clockwise and sometimes anti-clockwise. Similar to the throwing technique, one hand remains in the same position whilst the other shapes the clay. The bottom wall is pinched thinner, leaving clay at the top thicker for later shaping. Pieces are pinched out in stages, allowing drying times in between to avoid collapse. At leatherhard stage the pieces are scraped down in order to refine the form, leaving the base heavier for balance.

The use of colour has evolved from mixing oxides directly onto the clay to the application of slips and firing with salt. Coloured slips are painted onto the surface when the pot is dry and immediately polished with a stone, the brush randomly dipped from one colour to another without cleaning. Sometimes other clays such as brickdust might be sprinkled onto the surface and shaken off before burnishing again. A combination of cobalt, chrome, manganese, copper, crocus martis, iron plus nickel for brightening the other colours are used. The development of colour has been a mixture of repetition and experiment, the asymmetry of surface marking harmonising with the form and bringing it to life. Pieces are stacked one inside another together with salt, sawdust and seaweed (so that a local reduction takes place) and fired to 1000°C (1832°F). Owen talks about the magic of transformation caused by the fire and chemical reactions of the oxides and salt, the surprise of the unpredictable.

Research has shown that the right side of the brain is creative/intuitive and the left side represents the analytical/intellectual. The right side of the brain controls the left side of the body and vice versa. It is interesting that Owen, although right-handed, uses her left hand to pinch and form her pots but the right hand to perform the more

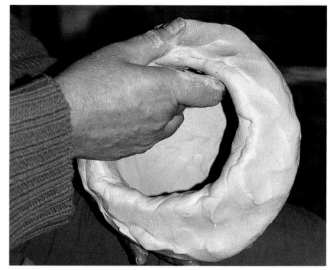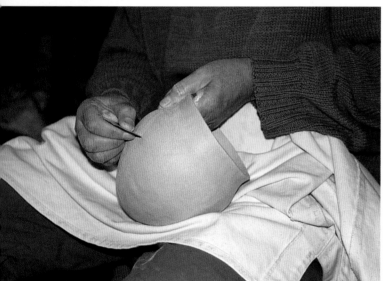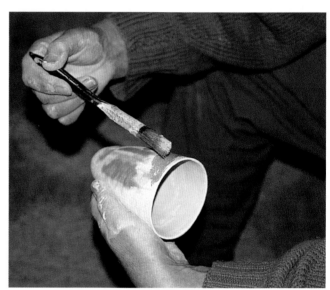

Making sequence (Top left) Pinching the hole in the middle of the clay ball.
(Top right) Pulling the clay upwards – the clay at the bottom has been pinched thinner, leaving clay at the top thicker for later shaping.
(Bottom left) Scraping and refining the surface with metal kidneys.
(Bottom right) Painting slips onto the dry surface. Photographs by Jane Perryman.

mechanical action of scraping with a tool. In order to be fulfilled, most of us need to use both sides of the brain – the creative and the intellectual. After our conversation about this Elspeth wrote to me:

> You know when you were here you talked about the idea that the development of my work in a more 'conceptual' direction might have to do with my wanting to use my intellectual side as well as the intuitive one. Well, I thought more about that and it seemed to ring true. And in addition I realised that it also connects to the political side; there is a part of

me that realises that making handbuilt pots in the 21st century is not exactly radical; whereas making mixed media work (with clay that is in a primitive state, e.g. wet with the handkerchiefs) I am getting more specific, dealing more directly with issues and other people. Generally being out in the world which is the other side of the inwardness of the pots.

Further reading

Coming Around Again, Elspeth Owen, joint publication by Elspeth Owen and Primavera, 1998

Nicholas Rena

I met Nicholas Rena in the late autumn of 2002 at his West London studio as he was preparing for his solo show at the Garth Clark Gallery in New York. It is always a privilege to see 'work in progress' – one begins to grasp the skill involved in the multiple processes which transform a piece from concept to gallery exhibit. As I entered the white room a mixture of angst saturated with ink fumes was physically tangible and hit me like a wall of hot air. There is a particular kind of tension ceramicists collectively experience as the fast approaching deadline of an exhibition looms closer. Is it going to work? Can I pull it off? Will it survive the kiln firing? Once the work is safely packed into crates the anxiety still remains of whether it will arrive intact. The pieces were lying on all available surfaces, some still naked white from the bisque and some already treated with layers of stain. Even in this state, amongst the detritus of a studio environment, their presence was evident. In the neutral clean space of a gallery they become powerful. Rena's fast-track journey from Royal College of Art graduate in 1995 to New York's most prestigious exhibition venue for ceramics is impressive and a result of his unique interpretation of form and surface as a dialogue between architecture and ceramics.

Combined with painterly Rothko-like surfaces of intense depths his work makes a potent statement in the world of contemporary ceramics. The forms are monumental with the precision and tautness of metal, their thick architectural walls setting up a dynamic between weight and volume. Emotionally, they seem to pull us in two directions; the desire to touch the polished surface of warm vibrating colour is rebuffed by the cool intellectual aloofness of the form. Rena talks about the influences of both modern and ancient art forms; his references to Abstract Expressionism through the painting of Rothko, and the classicism of early Egyptian sculpture:

> My last big shock was to visit Egypt in the last year of the RCA – I was struck by the sharp monochrome and stark sculpture. It's not pretending to be anything else but stone.

Nicholas Rena in his studio.
Photograph by Jane Perryman.

Educated at Eton and fortunate to have the 'ceramic spoon' of Gordon Baldwin as his teacher, he 'fell in love with everything to do with the process of making' to the extent of becoming Baldwin's apprentice from the ages of 14 to 18 years old. School was followed by a BA and MA in architecture at Cambridge University, which equipped him with an all-important sense of visual discipline. Although he was able to work on the new British Library and the Butlers Wharf development he missed the 'hands on' aspect of working directly with materials and processes. He told me how Alison Britton (his tutor at the Royal College of Art) would interpret his frustration with architecture as a lack of control – whereas working as a ceramicist would mean control over concept and production from beginning to end. During this architecture period, he also worked with steel sculpture when time permitted, but a desire to explore the containment of space naturally led him back to ceramic as a more appropriate material. Later, the crisp, taut qualities of steel would be transformed back into his ceramic forms. He attended adult education classes in ceramics and then went on to the Royal College of Art as a mature student. This was his third grant and he found himself at a disadvantage with his peers, who had come straight from ceramics BA courses and were much more focused and disciplined.

The pieces I made at the RCA were all over the place.

Rena's early work at 401½, his first studio, dealt with resolving two major areas of influence: the expressionist organic work of Gordon Baldwin and the machined intellectual work of Martin Smith. He continued with some of the techniques used

(Left) *Egyptian Eye,* l: 50 cm (19 ¾ in.), 2000.
Photograph by Michael Harvey.
(Above) *Asymmetric Bowl,* w: 45 cm
(17 ¾ in.), 1999.
Photograph by Andra Nelki.

(Opposite page) *Dark Jug,* l: 62 cm (24 ½ in.),
2001.
Photograph by Michael Harvey.

Making sequence
(Top) Making the prototype before casting in plaster.
(Above) The mould has been lined with compressed clay
55 mm (2 ¼ in.) thick.

at the Royal College of slipcasting very thick pieces characterised by sharp edges, monochrome and massive weight. He wanted to get away from his previous organic colour range and was experimenting with such materials as car oil to seal the bisque surface. By chance his girlfriend was playing with a bottle of blue-black ink to fill her fountain pen and accidentally spilt some – here was the solution.

It was a case of necessity being the mother of invention – I could use what was at hand to great advantage – it was cheap and required no spray booths or compressors.

He deliberately chose the vessel as his vehicle of expression, exploring jug and bowl forms which implied function while remaining elusive and statuesque. At an early exhibition in 1999 at Lynne Strover's gallery in Cambridge he said:

One is trying to make real those elusive qualities, the one natural and organic in appearance, the other artificial and machined. They both do have in common strong sculptural ambitions, ambitions disciplined by a commitment to the vessel as the controlling factor. I too am still trying to make the 'ultimate bowl' and the 'ultimate vase'. Of course it never quite works . . .

Rena has evolved a technique which is independent of the orthodox traditions of the artist potter. It is meticulous and begins with a technical drawing, planned to the last detail. Once an idea becomes resolved, the silhouette is drawn and a scale drawing made which is transferred into an MDF (medium density fibreboard) template. The initial shape is made from solid clay where he can determine the sharp line of profile, and then a multiple piece plaster mould is formed from the prototype. White earthenware clay is sliced directly from the bag and compressed into the mould in strips and layers to a thickness of 50mm (2 in.). After a couple of days the clay form is removed and slowly refined over a period of three weeks by scraping with metal kidneys, steel surform blades and razor blades. It is by painstakingly working the steel against the fine, leatherhard clay that the crispness and precision can be achieved. The final wall thickness will be about 35 mm (1½ in.).

After a slow drying out of six to eight weeks the pieces are fired to 1100°C (2012°F) over a period of four days. The bisque surface is sanded down with Wet and Dry sandpaper and then stained with three to six layers of coloured ink. The porous bisque soaks up the liquid, and by sanding and bleaching back the colour he can build up depth of tone just like a painter on canvas. Finally the pieces are polished with beeswax. Rena's use of colour represents the most intuitive side of his work – the rich reds are like well-nourished blood and the ultramarine blues like the depths of night sky or the ocean. Recently he has been using the solid flat colour of Farrow and Ball paint for some interiors 'to calm the piece down which is overloaded with nuance and detail'.

The forms have continued to develop around the theme of containment. An exploration of such domestic objects as spoons, ladles and open hands has metamorphosed into ritual objects. The recent work which he talks of as 'vessels made in anticipation' has associations with fonts and baptism (it is no coincidence he has just had a new baby) and a new orientation to a horizontal emphasis. These pieces have a narrow opening and elongate into a point; at the widest part of the form are two protrusions implying some kind of industrial mounting function. The strange lack of function, however, makes them even more elusive and suggestive. Rena talks about these pieces which lie on their side as 'less proud than the more active space grabbing pieces – as if something mysterious and incidental has just happened to them'.

Frederic Bodet of the Musée des Arts Decoratifs in Paris has said:

> His work seems to rule out any easy association with the cluttered reality of daily life. By definition an object occupies emptiness; through its simple but resonant presence, and through its weight – which is as visual as it is real – Rena's work dominates the emptiness around it. It establishes a 'ritual' which, in the purged space it makes, seems to redefine how one should contemplate an object.

Further reading

'Distance Imposée', Frederic Bodet, *La Revue de la Céramique et du Verre*, no. 117.

'Making it Work', Amanda Fielding, *Ceramic Review*, no. 192

'Nicholas Rena', Garth Clark, catalogue for Barrett Marsden Gallery, 2001

Lesley Thompson

Portrait of Lesley Thompson.
Photograph by Carol Topalian.

(Opposite) *Carved Vessel*, w: 30 cm (11¾ in.).

The optical designs on Lesley Thompson's classical pots contain references to both the traditional female crafts of textiles, basketry and pottery as well as the Op Art movement and the work of the painter Escher. Thompson lives and works in California and grew up in a family associated with the arts; her father was an architect and her grandmother a painter. She remembers visiting an exhibition of Op Art as a child and being deeply affected by the visual vibrations of black and white hard-edged patterns. Encouraged by her parents, she attended all sorts of art classes gravitating towards textiles which she continued to work with into her early adulthood. It is significant that her near-sightedness drew her towards the kind of focal concentration required for needlepoint and quilting. This attention to detail would later emerge in her ceramic work.

Thompson began her professional career as a book-maker and discovered ceramics late (at 30) via adult education classes. She was living in Australia at the time and attended a technical college where she learnt the rudiments of pottery making. Returning to California in the mid-1970s she took a workshop with the famous Pueblo potter Lucy Lewis and became interested in the designs and crafts of Native Indians. She says:

> I think the strongest influence has been the native arts classes I took in Idyllwild [California] with various Native American craftspeople in weaving, silver-smithing and pottery design. These classes confirmed my interest in surface decoration and it was from them that I learned that making art is a continuing process, rather than a product-making activity.

Lucy Lewis is now deceased but earlier this year I met her two daughters Emma and Dolores at their home in Acoma Pueblo. They still give workshops and in their quiet, bemused way told me the most important aspect of their art is to teach their students Thompson's point about the importance of organic development:

> We tell the people continually, 'Take your time, take your time.'

Time and patience are certainly at the core of Thompson's work; the linear grid systems which contain her design structures represent spatial time and the ingredient of patience is obvious.

Thompson works with a range of classical forms including narrow-necked bottles and open plates – but mostly with the kind of shapes we associate with Pueblo Indian pots. This is interpreted through many variations on a form which flares outwards from the base into a wide belly before sloping inwards again towards an opening. These forms act as blank canvases for their *raison d'être* which is to receive Thompson's hard-edged designs. Although the overall visual effect of the surface is highly controlled and graphic, upon closer inspection we can see clearly the hand of the maker. The carving is reassuringly human. Its change of direction, its change of pressure and the evidence of tool action leads to an unevenness of the white exposed porcelain which is emphasised by light and shadow. She says:

I like the feel of carving, I'm in love with it. The physical activity of the repetitive process has a meditative quality about it which I need.

Many of Thompson's patterns are based on the Navajo tradition of changing and reversing the design at the midway point so that the top mirrors the bottom. She also uses references to Amish quilt design and Maori designs from New Zealand. She says:

As I stretch designs inspired by various crafts over the curved surface of the pots, the patterns are enhanced by a new element – that of distortion. As I continue to study pattern styles from all over the world, I gravitate towards female crafts such as batik, quilting, weaving, basket-making and Pueblo pottery design. These process-orientated crafts have in common a continuous and extensive investment of time, as well as the need for careful hand skills.

Thompson describes her decision to adopt techniques which are painstakingly labour intensive, and require high levels of skill, as alluding to issues of gender. Historically, traditional female crafts have remained unrecognised and are still struggling to win the acclaim they deserve. She illustrates this point by talking about the Amish women who are masters in the art of quilt making but considered second class within their society.

Pots are thrown from porcelain and covered with black slip using a wide Japanese watercolour brush. Fine dental tools are used to inscribe the basic grid of vertical, horizontal and diagonal lines. The pattern is then carefully carved out with miniature curved knives, exposing the white porcelain underneath. The raised areas will

(Opposite) *Optical Checks*, dia: 38 cm (15 in.).
Photograph by Simon Chatwin.

(Above) *Carved Vessel*, w: 25 cm (9¾ in.).
Photograph by Simon Chatwin.

remain black during the firing. The skill to accomplish this level of freehand control is considerable, and Thompson compares it to the art of Chinese painting where a three-second gesture can take ten years to perfect. She talks about the need to be in a peaceful state of mind in order to avoid making mistakes and usually works at night when she can be sure of no distractions. Firing is to 1260°C (2300°F).

Lesley Thompson has been carving her pots for 20 years, which has led to carpal tunnel syndrome and surgery on her wrists. At this point she is investigating other approaches to her decorating. Although a physical restriction of any kind is devastating, it can also lead to innovative developments. The elemental desire to create is a powerful human force and usually finds a means of expression.

Making sequence
(Top) Inscribing the basic grid of lines through the slip.
(Bottom) The design is carved out with miniature curved knives.
Photographs by Simon Chatwin.

Mo Jupp

Portrait of Mo Jupp.
Photograph by Jane Perryman.

(Opposite) *London Lady,* ht: 30 cm (11¾ in.), 1996.
Photograph by Greg Preston.

On reading my notes from my conversation with Mo Jupp about his work a line jumped out from the page:

His love for women is what makes him tick.

Jupp's life experiences can be traced back for over 40 years through the narrative and themes of his ceramic sculpture. All the work is autobiographical, to do with his emotional response to events and relationships in his life, particularly to women. In the past he has said:

The subject matter that has occupied me since 1978, namely my attitude to the female, has remained fairly constant. The reason for this lengthy preoccupation is that I am always looking for better ways to describe what I mean. It is like a conversation that is not being understood. One changes one's tack and puts it in another way in the hope of making it clearer.

Twenty-five years later he remains absorbed in his search to find new interpretations for the female condition.

Jupp explores his subject matter through the language of stylised figurative imagery. He is a maestro of technical skill, enabling him to celebrate the seductive qualities of clay with great fluency, giving it the power to communicate directly. Jupp's work is not cerebral; he expresses himself instinctively though the heart and guts. It is rich in associations, with many cross-cultural references such as warrior helmets, Inuit shrines, dynastic handmaids and divinities, and African kingship staffs. However his ceramics are contemporary, instantly recognisable as his and very much about the present time. They are completely to do with his personal vision of the world. Like a photographer, he has the ability to capture a moment of human gesture and give it meaning by freezing it in time.

Jupp's early life in the 1950s was surrounded by people doing things – his father was a tool-maker, his mother a dressmaker. He used to watch her cutting out patterns and making garments from sheets of cloth. This would later become a literal starting-point for Jupp's

distinctive slabbing methods where he takes a flat sleeve shape and transforms it into three dimensions by folding and joining. As a young man, the experience of being conscripted into the army opened his horizons through contact with artists and architects, who encouraged him to prepare a portfolio and apply for art school. He was accepted at Camberwell in London initially for two-dimensional studies but was soon drawn towards the sculpture department where he was first introduced to clay. He remembers:

> Within one hour of working with terracotta I realised you could do anything with clay – you could make it and fire it a week later into something permanent. In sculpture it would take six months. The immediacy appealed to me.

The ceramic climate of the 1960s was dominated by the Leach tradition, but Jupp has always been a free spirit with a healthy disrespect for convention, and managed to avoid the throwing part of the syllabus altogether. (He later taught himself at the Royal College of Art.) However, the line-up of teachers there was legendary and he was fortunate to rub shoulders with Hans Coper, Lucie Rie, Colin Pearson, Ian Auld and Brian Newman. Within a few years Jupp had found his voice, winning recognition and acclaim at his graduation exhibition. Postgraduate studies at the Royal College of Art followed and since that time he has combined a career of teaching in many different art schools, including the Royal College, with studio work during weekends and evenings.

> I get great joy from them all and the added bonus of never feeling that I have a 'proper job'.

As a committed socialist he is passionate about education and has inspired countless generations of students through a combination of fierce optimism and dry humour – I remember his charisma when he taught at Hornsey College of Art where I was a student.

Jupp talks of having no personal life. This is because he has turned the personal into public through his art and teaching. The themes of Jupp's work are anecdotal and his storytelling skills of remembered incidents and conversations are riveting – they supply the raw material of his art.

(Above) *After Uglow,* ht: 15 cm (6 in.), 2000. Photograph by Norman Hollands.

(Opposite) *Figure*, 1997. Photograph by Norman Hollands.

In the 1970s he worked for three years with menacing helmet forms as a cathartic response to a near-death experience. He had fallen into the path of an oncoming car on the race track at Brands Hatch and in a flash saw the driver wearing a helmet and goggles. Miraculously he just missed being killed but the image of the driver turned into a recurrent nightmare which gradually faded through Jupp's ability to transform the trauma into something new. Next came a body of work on the theme of a container/box which outraged his audience at the Crafts Council where it was shown in the 1980s. This was Jupp's response to the constant use of sex in advertising and consisted of 'precious, private and very obvious' porcelain celadon glazed boxes containing gold/silver penises and

vaginas. Work followed containing references to derogatory male attitudes to women ('It doesn't matter what she looks like – put a paper bag over her head') and then pieces with a strong affinity to the elongated forms of Giacometti. During the early 1990s these static monumental forms changed, developing the characteristic of particular body language and becoming more gestural:

> I get 80% of my subject matter from Tesco's – that's where you see women. At the checkout they are bored and relaxed – unthreatened and accessible.

In the 1990s this intimacy of gesture expressed in his work became more detached again as Jupp explored the female form in the outside space of landscape. It became abstracted through 2-metre (6-ft) high vertical poles bearing a restrained indication of high breasts and was placed amongst meadows, woods and beside water. A body of work called 'Best Foot Forward' represented another interpretation of female portraiture containing humour and fetishistic overtones. Single feet supported by plinths were the results of Jupp asking various selected women the question 'Which foot would you put forward for me?' The male figure Icarus was investigated as another theme with references to Anthony Gormley's sculpture *The Angel of the North* and Jupp's memories of making model aeroplanes as a child.

Jupp's approach to his subject matter is to decide upon a title and then find the best way to express it, seeing it simply as a way to solve a problem:

> Mostly subjects offer themselves to me and I feel I must make some comment, state my attitude. This has to be in a three-dimensional way, that is what I do for a living. I have problems, I try to solve them, how doesn't really matter. I enjoy using clay more than any other material because I can manipulate it better, I can make it do what I want. I don't know if I am a sculptor or a potter, it doesn't really matter. I try to solve problems.

Jupp's work is all slabbed and is a celebration of clay as soft plastic material. Although it is enclosed one instinctively knows it is hollow and contains an inside volume. Jupp is very conscious of the quality of 'hollowness'. It is significant that when Jupp was at art school the catalyst for his interest in sculpture was seeing a fellow student carrying a bronze head with her hand *inside*. The realisation of 'space within' was the quality which first captivated him and continues to be a major concern.

Jupp's work retains a physical map of the clay's experience in its journey from amorphous lump to sculpture – we can see clearly his hand actions of rolling, folding, compressing, and joining. Jupp's skill is in allowing us to see this, of 'letting it all hang out' and making the stages important by revealing them. His work is like the preliminary sketch and finished piece all in one. We can also see evidence of the painting, rubbing and wiping of slips in between the multi-firings which come after the making

(Above) *Fragment,* ht: 35cm (13¾in.), 1999. Photograph by Norman Hollands.

(Opposite) *Gold Figure,* ht: 168 cm (66¼ in.), 1997. Photograph by Greg Preston.

Mo Jupp working in his studio. Photograph by Jane Perryman.

stages. Jupp's approach is versatile but generally he uses any stoneware or porcelain clay and after a bisque to 1000°C (1832°F) a white or black slip is applied (depending on the colour of the initial clay body) then wiped off before re-firing. This process is repeated many times until he is satisfied with the result before a final firing to stoneware temperature. Work is completed in limited editions around his themes and subject matter is constantly in demand and collected widely.

John Houston has referred to his 'glorious career' in the foreword to the monograph on Mo Jupp. He goes on to describe his 'ferocious aestheticism and virtuoso handling of materials'. There are few living contemporary ceramicists who warrant this kind of accolade but Jupp is one of them.

Further reading

'Solving Problems', Mo Jupp, *Ceramic Review*, no. 109
'Mo Jupp: New Work', Tanya Harrod, *Crafts*, no. 91
Mo Jupp, monograph published by Peter's Barn Gallery, 1997

Yo Akiyama

Yo Akiyama is a Japanese ceramicist whose sculptural work is concerned with the dialogue between three elements; clay, time and gravity. He says of his work:

Why clay? Why ceramic? What is creation for me? It is an important and endless question. But the expression of clay itself stimulates my imagination in the same way a stain on the wall can stimulate someone's imagination. Clay as material and ceramic as technology show me various possibilities. I can say that within each of my works are various answers to the question. Making ceramics is making stone. In my work I am saying that firing is the reduction of time or ceramics is the fossil of time. When I am engaged in the processes of making and firing I am aware of the element of gravity. Earth draws everything towards itself. But I hope to touch heaven. I think it is important to express the tension between the two different feelings.

Akiyama draws his inspiration from the natural world: rock strata exposed on a slope behind his studio, a spider's web, a wasp's nest, a shell, a slice of bamboo shoot, a deer antler. These forms in nature have a common principal of construction which determines how they grow and are shaped; their surface pattern indicating their internal structure. The surface is the point of exchange between the exterior and interior. Akiyama is interested in this relation-

Geologic Age 16, ht: 53 x 81 x 58 cm (21 x 32 x 22¾ in.), 2000. Photograph by Shigeharu Omi.

ship between the two and by literally turning things inside out the inside becomes the outside.

For Akiyama, the creative process is orchestrating the fissures in the clay as clues to interior events, and attaching meaning to the resulting shapes. A cylinder is thrown, cut and opened to turn its inside out. By passing the flame of a burner over the inner surface Akiyama can make cracks and crevices appear. The pieces are joined together to create a new form and, after drying, covered with a black slip then reduction fired to 1250°C (2282°F). Further treatment is through the application of iron powder and acids which after a few weeks will change to black or red or yellow.

Making sequence
(Above left) Removing the cracked sections of the cylinder.
(Below left) Deconstruction of the cylinder.
(Above) Creating a new form.
Photographs by Kazuo Fukunaga.

Ray Meeker

Ray Meeker is an American who lives in Pondicherry, south India. His background is in architecture and he is best known for his investigations and experiments into fired buildings. (A structure based on domes and vaults is built from raw mud brick, filled with raw ceramic products and fired so that the building becomes the kiln.) Meeker's ceramics combine architectural qualities of scale and containment with ecological concerns about the destruction of the planet. Recently he has used the head of an excavator bucket as a metaphor to represent the driving power of globilisation. The work is called *Kurukshetra* which was the battlefield in the story of the *Mahabharata* (the epic Sanskrit poem), and the splashes of iron are stencilled continents of the earth. The piece represents the earth as the battlefield. He says:

> Now the excavator bucket is becoming a common sight all over India, and again the politicians of the world have failed to treat global warming as the very real threat that it is. I make icons for the 21st century. Birdlike, the head of an excavator bucket – oversized – perched heavily between outstretched wings, conferring a mixed blessing, demanding a substantial human sacrifice. The bucket of the excavator – massive, voracious – for me embodies that momentum.

Kurukshetra, 183 x 122 x 107 cm (72¼ x 48 x 42¼ in.).

Anima Roos

Icarus, by Ray Meeker, ht: 84 cm (33 in.).

Anima Roos lives and works in Belgium. Her porcelain bowls have a tension between their classical delicate forms and the spontaneity of the brushed surface decoration. The pieces are thrown and then sanded and polished so that the turning rings are almost invisible. The surface is built up with wax resist and layers of thin slip before firing to 1240°C (2264°F) with a light reduction.

Porcelain vessels, ht: 15 cm (6 in.).

Meeker's large-scale work is handbuilt with a mixture of fireclay, wollastonite and grog, treated with porcelain and iron-bearing slips then woodfired to 1230°C (2246°F). Smaller-scale work is made with combinations of throwing and handbuilding from stoneware clay, treated with white and stained slips then woodfired to 1300°C (2372°F).

Further reading

'Perennial Earth, Quickening Fire', Deborah Smith, Cymroza Art Gallery catalogue, Mumbai, India, 2000
'Houses on Fire', Jane Perryman, *Ceramic Review*, Nov 1996

Opposite Page by Gunhild Aaberg:
(Above) *Part of a Circle*, ht: 20 cm (8 in.), 2000.
(Below) *Crossover*, dia: 165 cm (65 in.), 2000.

Gunhild Aaberg

Gunhild Aaberg is a ceramicist living and working in Denmark whose sculptural forms have qualities of both strength and fragility. Aaberg's work explores minimalist form and stark coarse surfaces divided by contrasting bands of colour. The work has some resonance with ancient artefacts and ritual objects. She says:

During my childhood I lived beside a harbour and spent my summer holidays sailing with a coaster. This life close to water, ships and harbours has inspired my work. I use references to the form of ships, the way they are painted and the visual signs associated with maritime life. I am also interested in contemporary tools and artefacts such as combination locks, remote controls and satellite dishes.

When I open the kiln and take out my pieces, I feel for them as I feel for a man. If they have something to say, I don't worry about small cracks and distortions – I don't want the work to be perfect. I want them to contain memories and associations with something elusive, to have a sense of mystery. These are qualities that you may not discover at first sight but which will slowly reveal themselves with time.

The work is made from heavily grogged stoneware clay using handbuilding techniques and then treated with black, white or red iron slips before firing to 1300°C (2372°F).

2 Clay Marked by Fire

This section presents a group of ceramicists who use the effects of fire on the clay surface. Although each person has an individual approach and achieves different qualities in their work, some of their concerns overlap. Direct marking by fire gives an immediate sense of depth where the effects of smoking or fuming penetrate deeply into the ceramic surface. There is often an element of unpredictability in the firings described here which is utilised and celebrated by these makers. Fire marks on an unglazed surface have an instant resonance with ancient pottery and so express qualities of timelessness. Where the clay is totally carbonised through black firing it can become mysterious and powerful as well. Burnishing or polishing the clay surface gives it a tactile, seductive quality and invites interactive handling or caressing.

David Roberts expresses both classical and elemental qualities in his vessel forms which are accentuated by the linear markings from a resist raku process. Sebastian Blackie uses the physical memory of flame touching the surface during saggar firing to express energy and drama in his work. Sometimes the performance of the firing itself is a vehicle for him to express specific concepts concerning his experience and response to life events. Petrus Spronk and I both use the burnished smoke-fired surface to express contemplative and tactile qualities in our vessel forms. Patty Wouters and Jimmy Clark use saggar and pit-firing with salts and oxides to achieve flashings of colour on the surface giving their work an association with ancient vessels.

(Opposite) *Burnished Vessels by Jane Perryman,* ht: 30 cm (11¾ in.), 2003. Photograph by Graham Murrell.

David Roberts

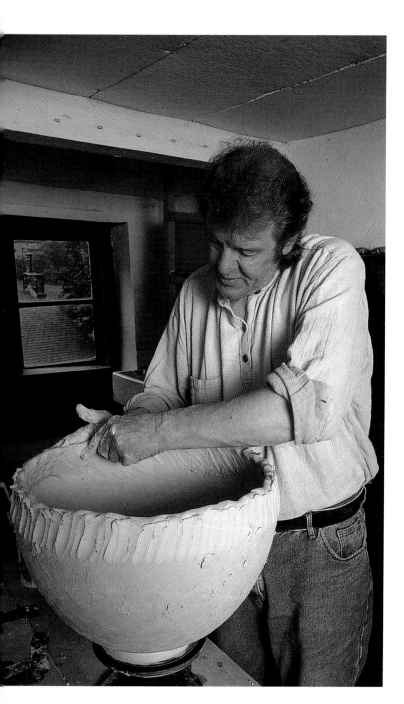

David Roberts in his studio. Photograph by Jane Perryman.

David Roberts lives in Holmfirth, a mill town which sits in a basin surrounded by the Pennine hills of Yorkshire. For the last 25 years his home has been a stone house, his studio on the second floor of the adjacent barn. From his window he can see the linear definition of stone walls dividing and tracing the contours of an undulating landscape. His studio is very bare, very simple and very clean. A well-scrubbed kitchen table of modest size, a small chair, a fireplace with a woodburning stove, a mantelpiece containing a row of stones. The chair and table look too small for such a large-framed man; but this is where he works, lovingly and painstakingly building his monumental vessel forms with coils of clay. These vessels are primarily concerned with volume, proportion and balance expressed through simplicity of line in both the form and surface. Over several decades, his work has developed into a highly sophisticated and refined ceramic art form. Talking about his work, Roberts says:

> People say, 'Why do you make pots?' Because I'm compelled to – life isn't right without it.

It is a privileged experience to visit an artist in his studio, his environment always giving further insight into the work. The surrounding landscape of gentle curves crisscrossed with lines has been absorbed into Robert's work, and underpins his aesthetic. The sparseness of his studio environment mirrors the classical purity of his form, whereas the modest table and chair give a poignant domestic resonance. Roberts came of age in the 1970s in the macho climate of the studio pottery course at Harrow School of Art with its emphasis on throwing. It was unusual for a man of his generation to choose the hand-building process of coiling. Coiling is a technique traditionally associated with women, the gender definition deriving from its lack of equipment and machinery, and the intimacy of repeated handling. Roberts was attracted to its simplicity and directness, of nothing coming between the maker and the made, and he talks of coiling as giving a quieter form. His approach is instinctive rather than intellectual; his work about judgement rather than measurement. His chosen technique certainly affects the presence and atmosphere of his work. He says:

> My ceramics are concerned with making the hollow vessel form which acts as a vehicle to bring to expression my ideas and feelings as an artist and human being. Landscape and nature give direction and orientation to my work. The linear patterns on the vessel's surface can be simultaneously a reference to rock strata, and an abstract means of exploring and articulating the complex interweaving of parabolic curves that make up the form of a coil-built vessel.

Roberts studied painting at Bretton Hall teacher training college in the 1960s, engaging with Abstract Expressionism, and responding particularly to the work of Rothko, Barnet Newman and Jackson Pollock where the canvas is treated as object. As with many ceramicists, he wandered into ceramics almost by mistake, studying it as a subsidiary subject and discovering that it suited his creative needs. He realised that, whereas painting requires subject matter, clay will justify itself. After teaching for a few years, he needed to be a maker again and started making pots on his kitchen table in a high-rise flat, carrying the work to his school for firing. The limitation of space led him into coiling by necessity. It is significant that he still works on a kitchen table, its intimacy helping to inform his work and connect it to its humble beginnings despite its highly acclaimed status. He has said of his work, in an interview with Jane Hamlyn:

> I have an intense, almost personal involvement with my objects during their making – a kind of primitive animism. Also, I believe that the length of time and almost obsessive handling involved in coiling impart a transferred intensity, an energy or presence in the work itself. I am concerned with the pot as archetype, volume and internal space expressing containment, inner life and mystery, held by the thin membrane of the clay wall. Circularity and roundness are potent symbols of resolution in a world of complexity and fragmentation.

In 1976 the American potter Jim Robison showed him some photos of American raku pottery which became an

important turning-point in Roberts' development. He had found traditional oriental raku uninspiring, but seeing the work of Wayne Higby and Paul Soldner opened his eyes to the monumental/sculptural possibilities of raku. The combination of intuition, spontaneity and controlled accident at the core of raku philosophy suited his intuitive approach. With the help of plans from an article in the American magazine *Craft Horizons* he developed a top hat kiln with a pulley system and counter-weight to fire his pieces one at a time. He became responsible for popularising raku in the British ceramic scene of the 1980s and 1990s. Another important source of inspiration was the work of Hans Coper, which Roberts first encountered at the Coper/Collinwood exhibition on tour in Manchester in 1969, the first time crafts were shown in a city art gallery. There are also references to the handbuilt Pueblo and Mimbres pottery where the forms are almost bursting through their thin skins and the painted surface decoration is imbued with spiritual meaning.

During the 1990s he became dissatisfied with the way the glaze rested on the surface of the form, representing a separation. He developed a raku technique where slip and glaze are removed after the firing revealing an integrated surface of black smoke marks which have penetrated deeply into the clay wall. He sees the lack of glaze as responding to the pre-industrial tradition, and of stripping away the veneer of sophistication.

Round Vessel with Ellipses, dia: 38 cm (15 in.), 1997.
Photograph by Jerry Hardman-Jones.

(Above) *Two Black Vessels with Lines,* ht: 27 cm (10½ in.), 1997. Photograph by Jerry Hardman-Jones.
(Opposite page) *Three Tall Vases with Ellipses,* ht: 60 cm (23½ in.), 2000. Photograph by Jerry Hardman-Jones.

Without glaze you're left with the fundamentals of fire and clay and what it will do.

The development of form in Robert's work has not been linear; he has explored many open and closed forms with a variety of references over the last 20 years. The open raku-fired bowls of the early 1980s were made alongside voluminous bottle forms with lugs and defined collared necks. During the 1990s he explored several themes inspired by Early Bronze Age vessels from Desmond Morris's book *The Art of Ancient Cyprus,* including *Basket Forms* with high looping handles and *Beaker Forms* with tall curved beak spouts rising from a bulbous base. Bottle forms were also produced at this time with flattened necks rising from rounded swelling bases. The earlier bowls developed into large flat dishes. In the late 1990s he produced a 'Vessel and Pedestal' series where forms resembling giant pebbles with their tops cut off sit on a flat slab form resembling the definition of its black shadow. Since the late 1990s Roberts has been exploring 'Tall Vessels' whose distinctive linear marking show clear references to rock strata. The *Vessels with Ellipses* are asymmetrical and slightly tilting, so that when grouped together a dialogue is created between the forms express-

ing an underlying anthropomorphism. The black smoke marking has been ground back to give muted grey lines resembling pebbles worn down by the erosion of water.

The clay body is a mixture of T-Material and porcelain. He uses extruded coils and builds the form up on a banding wheel, scraping the surface with metal kidneys to achieve symmetry. After applying a fine slip the surface is burnished before bisque firing to between 1000°C and 1100°C (1832°–2012°F). Like many handbuilders, he works with a 'family' of six to eight vessels, taking them all the way through the process over a period of six weeks. All his work is fairly big: in the range of 60 cm (23½ in.) high for the tall forms and 60 cm (23½ in.) diameter for the open forms, which relates to the width of his shoulders and his natural wrist/arm action.

After the bisque the surface is sprayed with a thick layer of slip (a mixture of 3 parts china clay and 2 parts flint) which will act as a barrier to the raku glaze. Next the raku glaze is applied and the design scratched through both the glaze and slip. During the raku firing of between 925°C and 985°C (1679°F–1805°F) the glaze melts and the pot is withdrawn at about 850°C (1562°F). After 20 seconds in the cool atmosphere, the crackle develops and the piece is placed into the reduction chamber with

sawdust. Carbonisation takes place as the smoke penetrates through and under the glaze crazing. On withdrawal, the glaze (aided by the barrier slip) peels off revealing the magic of smoke marks underneath.

Roberts talks about his work as a voyage of discovery, constantly needing to look for new directions. In her monograph on his work, art historian Lynn Green talks about how canvas and clay in their untouched state can be equally terrifying:

> The challenge of beginning a new form never lessens – in fact it is precisely this that keeps him going – it is his major motivational source. Like all true artists, Roberts needs the fear of failure in order to begin.

Further reading

Painting with Smoke – David Roberts Raku Potter, Lynne Green, Smith Settle, 2000

'David Roberts; Raku' Tony Birks, The Craft Centre and Design Gallery, Leeds 1990

(Top) *Large Bowl Form,* dia: 58 cm (22¾ in.), 2003.

Photograph by Jerry Hardman-Jones.

(Bottom) Detail of joining technique.

Patty Wouters

atty Wouters is a Flemish ceramicist who has chosen an investigation of archetypal vessel forms, sculptural elements and murals to express her ideas. For the last decade her work has gravitated away from domestic ware to conceptually based pieces often produced in 'series'. The titles such as *Moving Circles*, *Swinging Boxes*, *Swinging Urn* refer to movement, action or interaction and reflect Wouter's response to events in her personal life as well as to society at large. She has travelled extensively east and west to Japan, Korea, India, Indonesia as well as America through the world of ceramics, both to study museum collections of ethnographic and archaeological ceramics and to partici-pate in symposiums and workshops. She says of her work:

> Ancient vessels radiate a universal spirit. It is this kind of spirit I want to express in my work. My pots carry signs and symbols and tell stories about existence, relationships and communication, about origin and evolution. My intention is to allude to events and things that happen to humans in their private lives or in a broader social context. After all everything seems to be in motion and somehow connected.

Wouter's high energy has enabled her to juggle successfully not only a career in ceramics with fulfilling her family com-mitments, but also to pioneer and run an arts centre called Atelier Cirkel in Brasschat on the outskirts of Antwerp. Growing up as the ninth of ten children equipped her with a strong sense of drive and determination to make things happen – her enthusiasm and positivity is almost tangible. The family was artistic – her father conducted a choir and played the violin; her mother drew. Wouters remembers herself as a ten-year-old making constructions with sand and mud when the local motorway was being built. Later, after a year spent at art school in Antwerp, she took part in an exchange programme to Pennsylvania, America where

(Top right) Portrait of Patty Wouters.
Photograph by Jane Perryman.
(Right) *Floating in Blue,* ht: 8 cm (3¼), dia: 40 cm (15¾ in.).
Photograph by Katrin Daems.

she was formally introduced to clay and attended pottery classes. She found herself captivated with clay as a material but upon returning to art school realised she would have to study graphic arts (there was no ceramics department). She learnt the art of ceramics through evening classes.

The climate of idealism in the 1970s gave her a strong sense of social commitment towards education and for several years after leaving college she taught in schools. Later, she did a social work degree and became involved in social cultural work. She saw ceramics as a bridge between art and craft:

(Opposite) *Swinging Vases,* ht: 35/45 cm (13¾/17¾ in.).
Photograph by Katrin Daems.

(Below) Detail of wall panel *Hand – Talk,*
100 x 100 cm (39½ x 39½ in.).
Photograph by Katrin Daems.

When you make pottery it can serve as a piece of art but you can also use it. From this perspective ceramics is a more democratic art discipline – Is it art? Is it craft? That's what attracted me. I found the art scene too exclusive and wanted to find an art form more accessible to people. It's a personal attitude but has consequences in life.

Later, in the late 1980s and early 1990s she sought a new direction in her work (which had been mainly domestic ware), and began attending international workshops led by ceramicists such as David Roberts, Takeshi Yasuda and Antonia Salmon. She was inspired by the pure forms of Roberts and the meditative qualities of Salmon's sculptural ceramics. Wouters realised she needed to make a choice between the hard labour of production pottery and the development of more individual pieces based on ideas. The photo of a pit-fired pot in a book by Kenneth Clark captivated her and she started experimenting with low

Making sequence
(Top) Preparing for the saggar firing: wrapping the piece in wire wool,
copper wire, leaves and straw and sprinkling with copper sulphate.
(Bottom left) Pieces have been placed in the saggar with combustibles such as sawdust and
straw before partly covering and firing to between 600°C and 850°C (1112°F–1562°F).
(Bottom right) After the saggar firing, before unpacking.
Photographs by Jane Perryman.

temperature pit firing. The high breakage rate turned the experience into a kind of 'crusade' to overcome the many technical problems she experienced. During travels in the United States she met Bruce Denhert who specialised in pit firing and was able to illuminate the way forward for Wouters through exchange of ideas and advice. Never having been totally committed to glaze, she gradually changed her techniques from glazed stoneware and raku to an exploration of pit firing and saggar firing. Qualities resulting from the burnished surface and primitive firing techniques gave her the affinity with ancient pots which she loved. At the same time the galleries she dealt with encouraged and supported this new individual work. She had found her direction and has continued to explore the links between ancient pottery and life in the 21st century.

At first Wouters was primarily concerned with the process but as she overcame technical problems her concerns became more to do with self-expression. She talks about 'wanting to create the right atmosphere about the work'. She describes the ideas behind a series called *Swinging Vases*:

> Life is looking for the right balance between all its facets; like walking on a string – sometimes you're out of balance, so the work echoes this. The word 'moving' or 'swinging' – everything is moving on . . . your life . . . the days are moving – I wanted to express this.

Most work is made from porcelain, sometimes mixed with fine grog and/or stoneware clay for larger forms; the plaques are made from paper clay and smoke-fired. Basic forms are thrown, trimmed and burnished several times. Wouters enjoys the sensual feeling of throwing porcelain and compares the repetitive handling to a kind of meditation, giving her mental space. Additions such as complex feet or sculptural details are added, and when the porcelain is completely dry she applies several layers of terra sigilatta slip before burnishing again. Bisque is at

1040°C to 1080°C (1904°–1976°F) and then pieces are soaked in an iron sulfate solution to encourage more orange/brown colours during the saggar firing. When dry they are wrapped with copper wire and steel wool, then placed in a saggar with such combustibles as sawdust, leaves and straw. Copper sulfate is sprinkled liberally on and around the pieces before firing to between 600°C and 850°C (1112°–1562°F). The atmosphere of the kiln is somewhere between reduction and oxidation; if the saggars are closed completely the results will be darker.

Paralleling the development of her work has been her passion for the creation of a communal centre for the visual arts.

> When I started art school and studied graphics I had ideals of being an artist and sharing knowledge. I believed artists had to bring a message and confront the public with certain ideas. The other students did not share my ideals; they were afraid people would steal their ideas. I have found the world of ceramics to be much more open and generous spirited.

Like many successful ventures, Atelier Cirkel began humbly with a few volunteers offering a few classes. Over 15 years it has grown in size and reputation until now it consists of six spacious workshops offering courses in painting and sculpture as well as all aspects of ceramics together with a cafeteria and gallery area. Funding support from the Belgian government is facilitating Artist-in-Residence schemes and an International Ceramics Biennale event. Wouters has admirably fulfilled the ideals of her youth and combined them with her personal development as a ceramicist.

Further reading

Swinging, Patty Wouters, catalogue published by Artterre, 2001

'Joint Venture', Peter Lane, *Ceramic Review*, May 2000

Sebastian Blackie

Sebastian Blackie in his studio.

(Opposite) Sebastian Blackie's studio.
Photographs by Jane Perryman.

The overriding impression gained from visiting Sebastian Blackie at his studio in Hinckley near Leicester was one of paradox; of things not being what they seem. After initial hospitality he pointed through the window of the house into his garden, saying 'There's the studio I built.' I was looking at a wooden beach hut painted turquoise and ultramarine blue. Two glass-windowed cases set into the walls on either side of the door displayed a collection of coral and shells collected from a tropical beach. A bright yellow hammock was swinging on the veranda inviting me to relax and enjoy the sunshine; a pina colada would not have been out of place. Except this was a cold overcast day in early spring in middle England; it could start drizzling at any time. There were high privet hedges bordering the garden and the juxtaposition of suburban brick houses in the background. Standing on the veranda, looking back at his house, I felt as if I was participating in some kind of surrealist performance. It was a brilliant statement and a perfect metaphor for Blackie's approach to his life and work. By using the ambiguity of context he questions our perceptions and presents us with new realities. He has said of his work:

I am preoccupied with the paradoxes and tensions between our inner and outer lives.

Dyslexia (undiagnosed at the time he grew up) channelled his energies away from the academic towards practical skills and inventions. Growing up in East Anglia where clay is abundant he dug clay from the stream in his garden and made pots. From an early age his fascination with fire was there too; he remembers making bonfires and boiling water over a candle in a paper cup.

I tried to make my dreams work – the thing about learning is to be playful and use the knowledge one has accumulated. Learning can close play down.

After a Foundation Course with Zoe Ellison in Cambridge he wrote to Bernard Leach to ask advice about further study and it was suggested he go to Farnham – West

Surrey College of Art and Design. Amongst others he was taught by Mo Jupp and learnt the basic groundwork of pottery skills, becoming fluent at throwing. During a period of 20 years he was promoted from student to part-time teacher, full-time lecturer, Head of Ceramics and finally Head of Three-Dimensional Design. He was later recruited by Derby University where he now runs the MA course, Art and Design: Advanced Theory and Practice.

Blackie's life, teaching, writing and ceramic art hold equal importance for him. They are all integrated and underpinned by his basic approach of improvisation and playfulness which is expressed as a kind of performance. His experiments and success with paper kilns in the late 1980s and early 1990s were generously shared with the ceramic community through his articles (*Ceramic Review* nos. 115 & 130), demonstrations and workshops. An idea started by his Farnham students inspired him to develop a second kiln design made from tightly rolled newspapers twisted and plaited into rings to form a cylindrical structure around the raw pots. This research culminated in a three-week residency at Milton Keynes in 2000 where seven paper kilns of varying designs were built with the help of community groups, volunteers and local ceramicists.

Blackie is concerned with exploring how the value of ceramics can be communicated through activity and process, so that the making and firing of the paper kilns holds as much importance as the vessels fired inside.

Blackie's ceramics are a vehicle for his ideas and philosophy about the world and need to be looked at in this context. His work cannot be categorised as sculptural, ornamental or functional but serves to provide a structure in which an idea or experience can be articulated. He says:

> If we, as makers, wish our work to be understood, the burden of responsibility to ensure that our ideas are clearly articulated, not just strongly felt, lies with us.

Paul Vincent has described Blackie's work as raw and primitive, but at the same time urbane in character and carefully controlled; the work of an intelligent explorer rather than an artist of the commercial world. The drama of processes are potently celebrated in Blackie's work, expressed by the sensuality of wet clay and the movement of flame during firing. The finished work contains a flamboyance of gesture; every movement of his hand made permanent by the action of fire. Ceramics is a unique

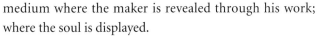

Making sequence
(Above left) Sebastian Blackie walks around a
stationary cone of clay while shaping it with
his hands, reversing the throwing action.
Photograph by Jane Perryman.
(Above right) Sebastian Blackie making paper/slip saggars.
(Opposite) Paper/slip saggars cooling in the kiln.

medium where the maker is revealed through his work;
where the soul is displayed.

He describes his piece *Millennium Mug:*

'Millennium Mug' reflects on the protocols of the
male public lavatory. I am interested in the ceramics
of the bathroom – the inevitable end result of the
ceramics of the kitchen and dining room. Marcel
Duchamp's urinal 'made' at the beginning of the
20th century continues to challenge us at the beginning of the 21st. The urinal is a fascinating artefact;
its shape reminiscent of female genitalia but the
preserve of the male. Public, nevertheless, the recep-
tacle of masculine intimacies that require heavy het-
erosexual comment in case one is misunderstood.

My mug/urinal is hand made, unique, attractive.
Its internal surface scratched with innumerable

signatures so dense that they become illegible – authorship is lost – toilet graffiti, the refuge of the disempowered. I wanted to make a very unsuitable 'mug' for the millennium.

Blackie uses a wide range of forming methods either singly or in combination, giving him the kind of versatility he needs. Nothing is fixed. His coiling technique is based on a Nigerian method introduced to him by Magdalene Odundo, his teaching colleague at Farnham. Some forms are produced by cutting through a solid block of clay with wire – a kind of three-dimensional drawing. Press-moulding is used where the mould is formed from clay covered with muslin to act as a separating barrier or from moulds constructed with paper. There is also the method of pulling – the same technique used in pulling handles – which he uses to make vessels. Recently while working in Japan he invented a new way of making where the lump of clay is positioned in the middle of a flat wooden batt and the maker walks around it backwards while shaping with the hands. This performance where Blackie becomes the wheel is ritualised through the repetition of motion into a kind of clay dance. Currently he is using unrefined dug clay and firing the pieces raw either in saggars – high temperature, 1280°C (2336°F) – or in paper kilns – low temperature, 760°–900°C (1400°–1652°F). Colour and tonal variation is a result of re-oxidisation during the firing. Saggar firing is not an exact science and not for people who require control over their results. It is a dramatic and seductive process where the physical memory of clay touched by flame remains evident, its unpredictability producing excited anticipation.

Through Blackie's connection with Galerie Besson in London he met Ryoji Koie who invited him to work at his studio in Japan. In the spring of 2000 Blackie spent six weeks working at Koie's studio preparing for an exhibition at Galerie Besson. He says of his experience:

> The work I made at that time formed a clay diary. A synthesis of incidents which, I think, might have gone unnoticed at home. When everything is new, everything is interesting. Tea bowls and urinals alike become part of a democratised value structure. I wanted to express my appreciation of Japan but was clear that Japan did not need another westerner

making oriental-style tea bowls. So stacked sake cups became drunken vases, tea bowls were joined to become larger bowls or stands and stools, reflecting the necessity of improvising with what is available in an unfamiliar environment.

Blackie describes *Stacking Tea-bowl Vase*:

During the 40 days I worked in Japan I was effectively denied speech for much of the time. It became strangely addictive. I learnt to listen and observe, to question myself more and others less. I tried to discipline myself to make with the minimum amount of material, space and effort; I used only as much skill as was necessary to communicate my idea. I approached the clay in the same way the Japanese approach food and worked with unprocessed clay dug from the mountain which maintained its rugged character.

'Stacking Tea-bowl Vase' reflects the experience of trying to make sense of an unfamiliar environment where all objects are potentially interesting. The 'vase' was the result of seeing a stack of tea-bowls on a shelf which I 'read' as one form. The adventure of travel is in self-discovery.

Goods is part of a series called 'Saki, Whiskey, Schnapps Cups' made for the Birmingham City Art Gallery Cultural Exchange exhibition for the festival of Japan in 2001. Blackie says:

'Goods' is based on the shape of the Japanese character for goods; two squares with a rectangle above, like a stack of cases. A pictograph. 'Goods' was made from many small thrown cups which have been tossed wet into packing boxes causing the individual cups to distort and fuse into a single mass. The series

(Above) *Millenium Mug,* ht: 23cm (9in.), coiled and saggar fired. Photograph by Sebastian Blackie.

(Opposite) *Stacking Tea Bowl Vase,* ht: 21 cm (8½ in.). Photograph by Sebastian Blackie.

of work is a melding of two experiences: a residency in Japan, which included a tour to Hiroshima's peace museum, and visiting the Holocaust museum in Sydney while doing a residency in Australia. It uses the fact that many cultures ritualise drinking as an act of hospitality, friendship and commemoration. The terrible beauty bestowed by the heat of the atomic bomb on domestic artefacts is linked to the image of the tangled, half-buried bodies in Belsen; an appalling consequence of a view of people as goods.

Goods is about the intractability of dealing with the unimaginable. The desire to forget and the difficulty of remembering.

Sebastian Blackie has been described by the editorial of *Ceramics in Society* magazine as 'the quiet radical of the ceramic world'. There are no boundaries between his life and work – all aspects are interconnected. Experience and emotion are expressed in his ceramic art, teaching and writing which in turn is an expression of his life. His passion is to be working with elemental materials and processes, to be engaged in the excitement of discovery and invention. It is his way of understanding the world.

Further reading

'More Paper Kilns', Sebastian Blackie, *Ceramic Review*, no. 130

'Use and Abuse', Sebastian Blackie, *Ceramics: Art and Perception*, no. 16

'Sebastian Blackie', Paul Vincent, *Studio Pottery*, December/January 1993/94

'Earth, Kiln and Fire', Marie Curbishaw, *Ceramics in Society*, Spring 2001, no. 43

(Above) Cup (one of 1000 installed in *Saki, Whiskey, Schnapps Cups*), ht: 5 cm (2 in.).

Photograph by Sebastian Blackie.

Jane Perryman

Some ceramicists find their direction early on in their careers. I was not one of those. Years after leaving art school, where I specialised in the industrial techniques of mouldmaking and slipcasting, I was still following all sorts of directions and searching for a way. While living in the United States in the early 1980s I was influenced by the 'Funky West Coast Ceramic School' from California and found myself casting porcelain vases formed from a mannequin's leg complete with stiletto heel. It can be amusing to look back 20 years at one's ceramic development. I wonder where all those porcelain leg vases are now – I wish I'd kept one.

A few years later, on returning to England, several factors culminated in a catalyst for change, enabling me to discover my voice. A friend, Elspeth Owen, showed me some of her burnished smoke-fired bowls. My intrigue was reinforced, as I had watched Siddig el Nigoumi (a Sudanese potter living in England) demonstrating his smoke firing at a ceramics festival in Wales the previous year. At about the same time I went to a retrospective exhibition of Hans Coper in the Sainsbury Centre in Norwich and was affected by the monumentality of his forms and the depth of his unglazed surfaces.

I wanted to simplify my approach to form and firing and made a decision to concentrate on handbuilding and smoke firing. I had always struggled with the alchemy of glazing and here was a way to integrate surface marks and decoration with the form. I liked the way the firing marks penetrate deeply into the burnished clay surface, giving a feeling of depth, and I liked the tactile element which invites handling and caressing. Pierre Bayle has said:

> Minerals leave me cold. For that reason I never make glazes. Glass cuts, it is rigid. It lacks life. I never manage to be moved by it despite its icy beauty.

His words had a resonance with the way I felt about glaze.

Clearing the studio of glazing and slipcasting paraphernalia was liberating. I loved the exhilarations and disappointments of learning through trial and error and became captivated with the endless possibilities of playing

Jane Perryman in her studio. Photograph by Kevin Flanagan.

(Above) *Burnished Vessel*, w: 40 cm (15¾ in.), 2003.

Photograph by Graham Murrell.

(Opposite page)
(Above) *Burnished Vessel*, width 39 cm (15½ in.) 2003.

Photograph by Graham Murrell.

(Below) *Burnished Vessel,* width 40 cm (15¾ in.) 2003.

Photograph by Graham Murrell.

with smoke. I began looking at unglazed pottery in the archaeological and anthropological departments of museums in London and Cambridge. Seeing the finger-prints on the work of a potter alive in 3000BC was a profound experience, and illustrates the importance of ceramics in the history of mankind.

My work has developed slowly due to my choice of techniques, together with the limitations of materials and studio space. Working for 14 years in a shed within a small town garden in Cambridge city gave me the kind of physical boundaries which can be frustrating but can also release creativity and generate ideas. The constraints which I often found frustrating focused my attention on develop-ing smoke firing in an urban environment. Using minimum tools and equipment I discovered various ways to fire combustibles in order to produce minimum smoke, and was able to achieve a whole range of smoke resists.

For the last six years I have been living in rural Suffolk where the quietness has enabled me to combine studio work with writing. In the research for this book I have conducted many in-depth interviews with cerami-cists, wanting to explore the 'why' as well as the 'how'. Inspiration behind creativity and how other aspects of life reflect and feed into ceramic expression can be revealing, increasing an understanding of the work. It is fascinating to look at the metaphors and analogies between life and work; to examine what feeds into what and the areas that overlap. I can see some of these connections between my own life and ceramics.

Burnished Vessel, ht: 28 cm (11 in.), 2003. Photograph by Graham Murrell.

For 25 years the practice of Iyengar Yoga has paralleled my work and development as a ceramicist. My guru B.K.S. Iyengar has made a comparison between yoga and art. He says:

> Any action done with beauty and purity and in complete harmony of body, mind and soul is art. In this way art elevates the artist. As yoga fulfils the essential need of art, it is art.

The Sanskrit word yoga means 'union of body and mind', which could be translated in ceramic terms as balance or the unity between form and surface, between inside and outside. The basic yoga pose is Tadasana (mountain pose) where we learn to stand up straight with perfect weight balance between the soles and heels, between the left and right foot. Alignment on both sides of the body enables us to lift and stretch up against the force of gravity. A yoga practitioner has to work with the limitations of the body and mind using its contradictions and weaknesses in order to achieve unity and harmony. As skill and under-standing develop and deepen, the practitioner can accomplish a level of 'effortless effort' – a state which is instantly recognisable whether expressed through music, sport, dance, ceramics, art etc.

In ceramics we start with the basic material of clay and need to develop skills to understand its qualities. Michael Cardew has said:

> The difficulties and natural obstacles presented by the technical sides of the potter's art are themselves a potent source of inspiration.

Once the basic skills are mastered the ceramicist can go on to explore ideas of form, surface and context. It is a continual dialogue between ideas, constraints and possibilities. Unlike other art forms, ceramics is eclipsed by the limitation of the firing with all its hazards and risks.

During the last 18 years I have used the vessel as my basic form, exploring its possibilities gradually so that one idea develops organically from another. My approach is mainly intuitive. From time to time I use formal plans and drawings which can be useful as a guide but I find a two-dimensional idea always needs to be considerably adapted in its three-dimensional reality. My current work explores the element of ambiguity and the dynamic of opposites. Ambiguity is expressed by the exploration of weight and volume through the use of double walls, so that the pieces appear solid but when held are surprisingly light. The slow controlled making and burnishing contrasts with the drama and unpredictability of the firing where some element of surface marking is anticipated but not predicted. Underpinning the work are universal opposing forces of symmetry/asymmetry; of inside/outside; of curved/flat; of horizontal/vertical; of masculine/feminine.

There are many analogies between a vessel and a human body; we refer to parts of a pot as foot, belly, shoulder, neck. There is a relationship of the inside to the outside or the soul to the physical shell; of the structure to the surface or the skeleton to the skin. The clay vessel, just like the human body, can be made open, closed, soft, taut, dynamic, powerful, vulnerable or surrendering, taking on these characteristics from its beginnings as plastic clay. In this way, ceramic form can express emotion. After many years using narrow-based, flaring forms which generate feelings of lightness and optimism, I am now investigating its antithesis. Round-bottomed forms express qualities of security and being well grounded, and although they balance on a tiny point, will rock but cannot fall over. The flatter slabbed pieces have gentler curves and sometimes support the bowls. Where the two pieces are presented together, the bowl can be re-positioned or tilted, inviting a different tension of balance and a new interaction of curved lines. There are references to the Zen meditation bell which sits on a cushioned platform, waiting to be 'invited'; the practitioner picking it up and striking it to facilitate awareness. Sitting on a platform gives the bowl form another context and a new significance of formality. I am interested in the viewer engaging directly with the piece through the action of reaching out and picking up, of handling and re-arranging.

The pieces are handbuilt using combinations of coiling, press-moulding and slabbing techniques from a mixture of T-Material and porcelain (in the ratio of 2:1). A porcelain slip is applied before burnishing and then fired to 1000°C (1832°F). Some pieces are treated with resists (paper, wax and clay slip) then saggar fired with sawdust to around 700°C (1292°F). Other pieces are smoke fired in oil drums or brick containers outside so that the firing is partly oxidised, giving greater tonal contrast than the saggar firing.

I live with a jazz musician whose main concerns are with improvisation, whether applied to performance or composition. The dictionary defines improvisation as 'to perform or make quickly from materials and sources available, without previous planning'. Hans Coper has compared the art of ceramics to the playing of jazz in its constant improvisation on a theme. This improvisation with the elements of earth, fire and water is what motivates me to continue searching for new ways.

Making sequence (Left) Preparing a saggar with layers of sand and sawdust.
(Right) Removing the piece from the saggar after the firing. Photographs by Jane Perryman.

Tjok Dessauvage

Tjok Dessauvage is a Belgian potter who has won international recognition for his distinctive sculptural vessels which use a double-walled throwing technique. He began his career in ceramics making functional ware, but for the last 20 years has been exploring and developing a more sculptural approach. He describes his work:

Some 20 years ago I started to work in a new way making non-functional forms, still thrown. My aim was to make massive-looking pieces. After many experiments I developed the technique of double-walled or reverse throwing, firing first raku before changing to terra sigillata, a technique I had experimented with many years before. From the formal point of view I restricted myself to archetypes like hemispheres, conical forms, cylinders and a flat form derived from old millstones. With regard to technique I mainly used clay and smoke and the decoration on the pieces became minimal. Each pot is considered as a kind of small-scale universe incorporating an energetic pattern, trying to give a perfect finish to enhance the austerity and feeling of loneliness. The flat upper surface is the bearer of the message and gives the piece its own vitality.

My sources of inspiration originate from a wide field and include certain abstractions of landscapes, elements of nature or spatial orbits. Codes such as electronic schemes, architectural plants or even sewing and embroidery designs are used as starting points, as well as narrative decoration, patterns of pottery or archaeological fragments. Photographic and printing techniques are used in order to obtain exact duplicates of these relics, a kind of remains of energy. In other pieces, the basic structure is broken by cutting a fragment out of it. The isolated piece receives its own vitality. A bond with the original

(Above) *Orbit,* ht: 20 cm (8 in.), dia: 28 cm (11 in.).

Photograph by Hans Vuylsteke.

(Opposite) *Magic Square,* ht: 10 cm (4 in.), dia: 45 cm
(17¾ in.). Photograph by Hans Vuylsteke.

structure remains to a greater or lesser extent. In this way formal aspects become subordinated to the created situation.

Dessauvage's concerns to bring the wealth of everyday experiences into his work is matched by his versatile approach to technique. Through the limitation of his forms he has developed a broad personal vocabulary of clay processes which are improvisations on a theme. They have been described as 'Three-Dimensional Haikus'.

He uses a variety of clays – both stoneware and earthenware – to which can be added coffee grounds, perlite or vermiculite to obtain a more sculptural surface. Etching techniques are sometimes used: thermal etching, where a small burner is passed over the leatherhard clay, causing it to flake off, and vinegar etching where vinegar is painted onto the dry surface to achieve a volcanic look. Drilling holes or inscribing lines into the leatherhard surface are other approaches to divide and mark the surface. After the forms are thrown the terra sigillata is applied and then polished. Dessauvage uses a variety of firing methods and firing temperatures to achieve different effects but basically he uses an initial oxidised bisque between 900°C and 1150°C (1652°–2102°F) followed by a heavy reduction firing with sawdust or wood. The principal is that higher temperatures will give the terra sigillata less porosity and control the absorption of less or more black smoking.

Further reading

'Attention to Detail', Tjok Dessauvage, *Ceramic Review*,
    no. 200

Petrus Spronk

Petrus Spronk was born in Holland but has lived in Australia since 1957. After graduation he travelled extensively in Europe and America, and these experiences together with an interest in Buddhist religion have helped to inform his work. Spronk restricts himself to the forms of burnished open bowls which lift up and swell out from a small base, and investigates aspects of surface design through the application of gold leaf. His introduction of ceramic as a material of paradox is presented through the bowls which have been broken and reassembled into a whole. These pieces contain shards which remind us both of the breakability and devaluation of ceramics as well as the preciousness associated with gold and the value of something made whole again. The quality of his work is basically restrained and minimalist, containing a sense of meditative stillness. The pieces are objects for contemplation. He says of his work:

> For most of my life I have worked in relative isolation and solitude. Although this was important it also had its difficult aspects. Difficulty in continuously testing myself for excellent work. Difficulty in not being able to share with others. Difficulty in not relating my work to others to see how it was going. However, despite these difficulties, the solitude was necessary for the creation of the spirit of my work.

The pieces are thrown, turned on the wheel and burnished. Some bowls are decorated through etching and some broken at this stage, with consideration as to the number of shards required to make a satisfactory composition later when the piece is restored. Spronk has built a wood-fired kiln on the side of a slope in the ground where he carries out the bisque firing to 900°C (1652°F). After a black firing the gold leaf is applied and the broken sections of shard are re-assembled to re-form the bowl. Spronk talks about his inspirations coming from many sources as diverse as fashion and car design to the landscape after a bush fire or Islamic architecture. He says:

These works are the result of my physical interaction with shapeless lumps of clay and a wood-fired kiln. Additionally, there have been many subtle influences in my life, which have carried over into my work and may, at first sight, not be too obvious. There have been many friends and many meetings. There has been a total commitment to this work. There has been, and is, much spirit and soul. There are many stories and memories. And, as an underlying strength of all this, there is the love for the simple act of using my hands to make something beautiful.

(Left) *Black Bamboo Grove. Movement in stillness, Power in Silence,* ht: 21 cm (8½), w: 32 cm (12½ in.).
Photograph by Alison Pouliot.
(Below) *Moon reflection. As Above, So Below,* ht: 12 cm (4¾ in.), w: 18 cm (7 in.).
Photograph by Alison Pouliot.

David Jones

David Jones uses black firing and raku to investigate the heritage of Japanese 'tea ceremony' vessels and their re-interpretation. He refers to the work as 'Deconstructed Tea Bowls' and says:

> This body of work is concerned with the creation of a vocabulary, of form and surface, through contrast. The pieces reference bowls, the archetypal form of ceramics. They are about containment, both in the volume of trapped air in the double wall and the shallow depression that could hold. The architecture of the bowl is confronted to generate a grammar of shape. The inside is related and contrasted to the outside profile. Free marking on the interior, gouged with rough tools, a machined finish on the outer skin, all reflecting the range of texture made possible with the rotating potter's wheel. Between these two surfaces lies the rim, which is also seriously considered, as the significant interface between the outer and inner realities.
>
> This treatment focuses on the softness, the pliability and the way in which clay can take up an imprint and be manipulated when plastic. In this way it recapitulates its own geological history – from mud to rock. The work takes as its influences the vessels of the Japanese Tea Ceremony – in particular the tea bowl. This is further informed by my own take on the references of the Japanese masters – the impressions and markings left by the abrasions of the sea, to the systematic dragging of plough across countryside.

Three Raku Fired Vessels, 25 x 14 cm (9¾ x 5½ in.)
Photograph by Rod Dorling.

The relationship of the ceramics to the human body is very significant, both in terms of scale of the work and in the idea of skin and the intimate marks found in the crumpling of flesh.

The work is made either by using a fine porcelain clay, or a porcelain clay mixed with molochite, because it is so responsive as a register of these traces. It is then either vitrified or raku fired, the latter pots removed red-hot from the kiln and either buried or fumed in sawdust to allow varying degrees of penetration and marking by carbon. This gives a product that is soft and warm to the touch, in contrast to the bony hardness of the high-fired pieces.

Jimmy Clark

Jimmy Clark lives and works in America and is known for his pinched organic vessel forms which are sawdust-fired with salts and sulfates. He says of his work:

My forms are mostly inspired by pottery from various ancient cultures: Latin America, China, Greece (particularly Crete) and Egypt. I find a commonality in the simple elegant forms of these ceramic traditions that possesses a universal appeal and bridges cultural differences. In my work I attempt to connect with this spirit and purity of form. I approach the creation of these forms with an intuitive understanding as opposed to a cerebral preconception.

I employ almost exclusively the ancient hand-building technique of pinching, and restrict myself to forming the piece out of a single ball of clay. I rarely begin with a preconceived notion of desired shape, but rather allow the vessel to grow into its final form. The piece is formed on my lap or in 'nests' that I make by loosely spanning a towel on a bucket. I interact with the clay, allowing the consistency of the material to contribute to the ultimate shape of the pot. I then either burnish the piece with hard, polished, semi-precious stones or apply terra sigillata which I then buff polish with a soft rag.

This method is extremely slow and time intensive. Some of my larger vessels require 40 to 50 hours work, and up to a month to finish. My semi-improvisational approach is completed through my preferred firing method of sawdust or pit firing, which blackens the pieces in totally unpredictable and uncontrollable ways. Recently I have begun using salts and sulfates in the firings which fume the work with splashes of colour – the pieces and surrounding sawdust are sprinkled with table salt and copper and iron sulfates. I have also experimented with wet newspaper 'wraps' where I sprinkle damp newspaper with salt and sulfates and then wrap the pot before placing it into the sawdust firing. I have begun experimenting with the application of terra sigillata to bisque ware which often peels off in the fire. After scraping and stripping the surface of the vessel a singularly rich and varied surface remains, resembling spider webs intertwined with cartography.

I find that these more varied surfaces increase the sense of 'history' for the vessel. The desired result is timeless mystery, a sense that the pot has had a long life of its own, independent of its creator. Despite the many techniques that I have begun to use in my firings, the supreme joy of the method is its ongoing unpredictability and refusal to be controlled. I think of myself as but one of three integral elements that share equal responsibility for the creation of the work: artist, material, and fire.

(Left) *Amphora,* ht: 46 x 12 cm (18 x 4¾ in.).

Photograph by John Carlano.

Jill Solomon

Jill Solomon lives in the United States, although she was born in South Africa, and brings to her work some of these cross-cultural references. Her organic sculptural forms have strong connections with rocks and pebbles which are further emphasised by the surface marking achieved by saggar firing. She says of her work:

> I was born in South Africa and my roots in that country run deep. I carry vivid memories of its sights and sounds and smells and, more particularly, of African women walking through the long grass with large bundles on their heads or babies on their backs. They wore brightly coloured clothing and beaded jewellery emphasising long necks and natural elegance and dignity.
>
> In my early childhood I was surrounded by African women who had a profound effect on me. They gave generously of their love, and their capacity to transcend their own personal and political suffering to offer compassion to a child of the persecutor always amazed me. These sculptures are a tribute to the African women who gave me so much.
>
> I am very drawn to the art of Africa as well as the early Palaeolithic and Neolithic sculptures of old Europe. My goal is to make work that reflects both the simplicity and essentialness of this art while at the same time bringing this influence into the contemporary culture in which I live. The beauty (and difficulty) of the saggar firing technique which is serendipitous to a large degree ensures that no two pieces will be alike. It gives a richness of design and colour that is meant to enhance the simplicity of the form.
>
> Ultimately, it is important to me that my work conveys the connection I feel with the clay and the kiln and the immense pleasure that this relationship brings.

Pieces are handbuilt from low-fire white or red earthenware clay and covered with terra sigillata slip before polishing. During the bisque firing to 980°C (1796°F), copper wire of varying thicknesses is laid onto the surface which will leave distinctive lines after the firing. A saggar firing follows where the bisque ware is surrounded with sawdust and salt marsh hay which has been soaked in oxide solutions (red iron, cobalt, copper and yellow ochre). The hay can also be wrapped around the forms and secured with string. The firing proceeds slowly to around 830°C (1526°F) followed by a light reduction for 15 minutes before turning off.

Compassion, 38 x 15 x 7 cm (15 x 6 x 2¾ in.), 2001.
Photograph by David Caras.

Duncan Ayscough

Duncan Ayscough's thrown vessel forms have strong historical associations, both in their forms and seductive terra sigillata surfaces. He says:

My pots seek a balance between the precise structure and control of throwing and turning on the potter's wheel and the fiery chaos of the smoke firing. These elements combine in the production of the finished pots – form and surface. The pots, which have withstood the rigours of the making process, are witness to the united creative power of the maker and fire. I look at people as if they were pots and vice versa: physical structures that contain an intangible life force, fragile objects, yet hardened particles from the earth – eventually returning to it.

On the land rising up behind my home in Bethlehem, west Wales, is the huge Iron Age hill fort of Garn Goch, which incorporates a 4000-year-old Beaker People burial mound. In a nearby field are remains of a Roman villa. My research into terra sigillata introduced me to other cultures, including pre-Columbian pottery, Egyptian funerary jars and glass Islamic tear jars. These links with earlier cultures influence my work through an awareness that ceramic artefacts provide some of the strongest physical links between distant cultures and our own time.

My pots are thrown from fine white earthenware clay, often in two sections which are joined together at the leatherhard stage. Several layers of terra sigillata (with a high soda content to encourage crazing) are then sprayed on before a bisque firing to 1000°C (1832°F). After the bisque it is possible to see if a pot has developed a crazing in the terra sigillata surface which will hopefully show as dark linear spirals during the carbonising. Next a long slow sawdust firing takes place in a metal container using hard and soft woods for different results; hardwood provides an intense surface whereas softwood burns faster providing a more dynamic movement of the carbonisation across the pot. On the interior of many pots I use 24 carat gold leaf, taking pleasure in the contradictions of

Long Necked Pot, ht: 33 cm (13 in.), 2000.
Photograph by Duncan Ayscough.

combining two materials which both have a long shared history with human civilisation; one very humble and the other highly exalted.

The control and chaos of the process can make for an agonising combination of heartbreak and euphoria. The precise control of making and applying surfaces is sacrificed to the chaotic uncontrolled 24 hours of the pit-firing process which can literally make or break a pot. It is this potential for serendipity and the ultimate unique individuality of each finished piece that keeps me enthralled and creating ever more pots in striving to achieve the unobtainable ideal.

Violette Fassbaender

Violette Fassbaender

Perceptions of Depth and Reflection, dia: 45 cm (17¾ in.), 1996.

Photograph by Reto Bernhardt.

(See chapter 4, p.144 for an explanation of her work.)

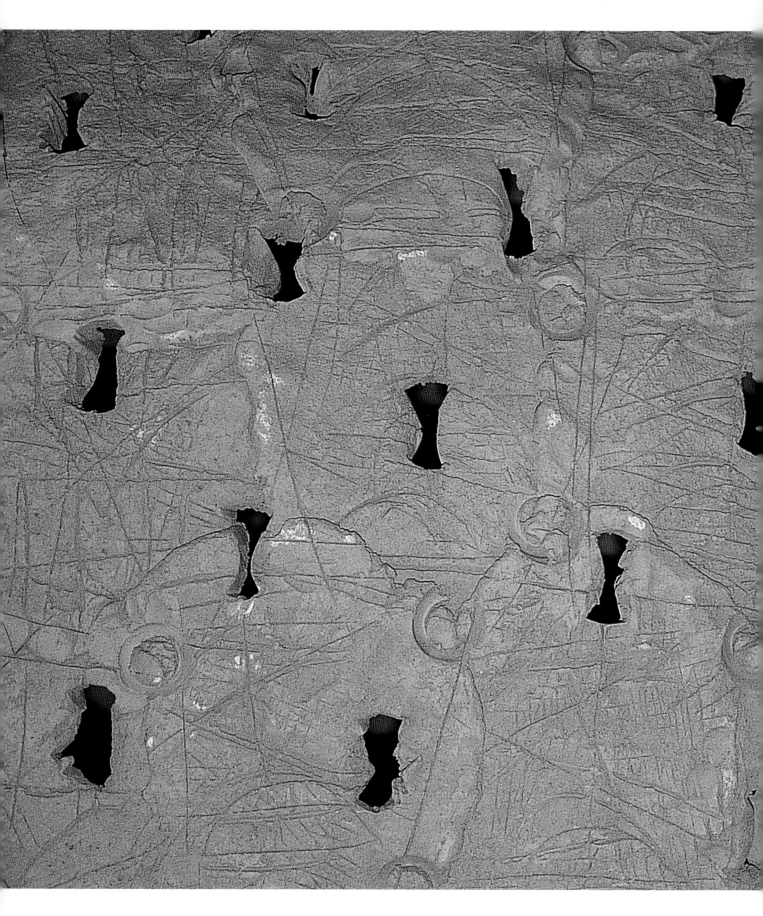

3 Pure Clay

The diverse work of ceramicists in this section reveals the qualities of pure fired clay without any additions. The element of light is also an important factor, presented either in the translucent properties of porcelain or through pierced holes in the clay surface. The ceramics featured here include delicate translucent bowls, site-specific sculpture, installations expressing the paradox of clay as a material of limitation, and porcelain light sculpture where electricity allows the light to be thrown outwards beyond the form.

Arnold Annen has refined his cast porcelain bowls to their very limit of translucency, contrasting the highly-controlled making with a spontaneous approach to surface treatment. His thick-walled sculptures have been embedded with pieces of charcoal which burn out during the firing, allowing light to travel in and out. Philippe Barde uses the properties of slipcast porcelain in his instal-

lations and vessel forms to push the physical boundaries of clay and so challenge our perceptions. Alison Gautrey exploits the translucency and delicacy of porcelain through her unorthodox technique of spinning whilst casting. Margaret O'Rorke retains the seductive fluidity of thrown porcelain in her light sculptures which allow the light to radiate within and without. Lawson Oyekan uses a red firing clay to build his monolithic sculptures which possess an elemental spiritual power concerned with transformation and healing. The surface is broken up with calligraphic scratching, textures and slashed holes which allow the light in and out. Although Satoru Hoshino's work was originally black fired, I have included him in this section as much of his large scale work since 1998 has been built from a black stonewrae clay fired in an oxidising atmosphere. His installation sculptures express a powerful metaphor for the universal destructive force of clay as matter.

(Opposite) Detail of surface, Lawson Oyekan.

Arnold Annen

Arnold Annen in his studio.

(Opposite) *Archaeodictyomitra II,* l: 220 cm (86¾ in.), dia:75 cm (29½ in.), 1998. Photograph by Reto Bernhardt .

There is a startling portrait photograph of Arnold Annen for an exhibition catalogue at the Museum of Art in Geneva by the Swiss photographer Nicolas Faure. Annen has been caught at the moment of transporting a batt supporting a large thrown section for his ceramic sculpture. The slightly flaring cylinder is held up at shoulder height, tilted at an angle, completely obscuring his face. The photo has been cropped so that we see his waist, his upper torso, one arm and two hands holding the batt. It is a reminder that ceramics bares the soul of the maker; whether or not we see Annen's face, he is instantly recognisable through his work.

Arnold Annen is a renowned Swiss ceramicist, with an international reputation for his work in porcelain which has won several prestigious prizes in Japan and Europe. His reputation grew alongside the development of his thrown porcelain bowls whose wafer-thin walls and translucency were taken to unknown levels of expertise. Watching a video of Annen's working methods (shot without verbal text at a residency in Japan) is akin to watching a dancer's performance; each process engages the concentration of his whole body and becomes significant in its own right. Since 1993 Annen has paralleled his vessel work with large sculptural forms which investigate the elements of form, space and light on a different scale. He says of this work:

> My desire is to experiment deeply with the relationship between the object in its environment through space and light.

Annen comes from a family of farmers and carpenters, growing up in Gstaad, a mountainous area between Bern and Geneva. From a young age he became familiar with tools and processes and remembers digging up local clay and building a pottery wheel from a car tyre and plate. This kind of learning through play was encouraged by the Steiner school he attended and the kind of enlightened teaching that integrated art and philosophy into everyday lessons. Annen's work today is underpinned by many years of disciplined, rigorous training which he sees as a series of steps, each one preparing for the next. He began with a four-year

(Above) Porcelain bowl, ht: 13 cm (5¼ in.), dia: 21 cm (8½ in.), 1999.
Photograph by Reto Bernhardt.

(Opposite) *Light and Space Interaction,* l: 35–95 cm (13¾–37¼ in.), dia: 75 cm (29½ in.), 1996.
Photograph by Reto Bernhardt.

traditional apprenticeship to become a production potter – where he learnt to throw 200 pots a day – followed by a year in Geneva with the potter Jean Claude de Crousaz.

Annen's fascination with wood firing took him next to La Borne in France where he spent three years learning the art of wood and salt firing under the guidance of Pierre Mestre. There he met a Danish potter Sten Keep who invited Annen to accompany him to Japan to study Bizenware. This turned into a three-year stay, working with a family of traditional Bizen potters where he learnt the subtleties of wood firing and a different approach to aesthetics from our European way of seeing. He says:

They didn't like my throwing technique – I made 500 saki bottles, carefully trimmed, turned and signed and when I asked them what to do with them they said 'Throw them away and start again.' The main thing I was learning was about the texture – in wood firing there is no glaze so the throwing is important – it has to be perfect but not too perfect – the edge has to be uneven but not too uneven! The philosophy of perfect imperfection. It was an important time – it made me think in a different way. At first I didn't understand but finally I began to think about the unique character of each piece. I was very dedicated and focused – I spent three years in the village without going home. At the end they allowed me to make my own work and have my own exhibition.

From 1980–84 Annen set up and ran his first workshop near Brienz in Switzerland, making a range of celadon, tenmoku and copper red glazed stoneware for tourists. It was a success commercially but his heart was not in it and when the opportunity arose to house/studio sit in Amsterdam for the Dutch ceramicist Barbara Nanning, he took it. This was an important turning-point in Annen's career, as it was here that he 'found his voice' after the many years of travelling and gathering expertise from different ceramic traditions. He began to make colour tests with porcelain which developed into an exploration of the art of neriage (a section is cut out from thick bowl, filled with coloured clay then re-thrown to take the contrasting colours into a spiral). The success of this work (he won a major prize) was cut short by circumstances, which forced him to abandon it. The gas kiln he built was transported to Switzerland where a different pressure system resulted in different colours. In 1990 Annen set up a studio in Basel with his partner, the ceramicist Violette Fassbaender whom he had met in Japan. He began a new challenge of taking thrown porcelain to its limits of thinness and translucency, each piece requiring four hours throwing and eight hours trimming.

At a symposium in Kecskemet, Hungary in 1996 he began experimenting with slipcasting, exploring and developing many techniques to avoid the visibility of forming marks. The highly-controlled forms flaring out from a narrow base are given relief by the spontaneity of a surface freely brushed with layers of slip. The quality of light and depth is able to constantly change inside and out as the bowl is turned. The use of a gas torch to facilitate drying led to an accident where the surface of the bowl dried too fast and broke up. Many inventions and developments occur in ceramics as a result of mistakes and Annen had the intelligence to explore what had happened and develop it – leading to yet another prize.

In 1993 he was invited to exhibit in a large church basilica at Châteauroux in France. The inspiration Annen experienced from such an enormous space became a catalyst for the beginning of his site-specific sculpture.

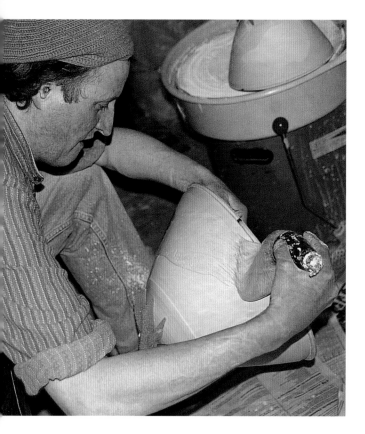
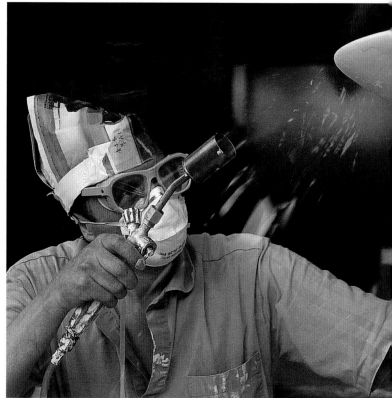

Making sequence

(Above left) Slip decorating with a chinese brush onto a raw bowl.
(Above right) The leatherhard bowl is treated with a gas burner to cause explosions on the surface.
(Opposite) Working on *Stichyomitra II* in Japan 2002. Small slipcast cones are attached to the main body.

This departure from the vessel has enabled him to show his sculpture in contemporary art exhibitions and taken his work to a wider audience. He describes his underlying concept:

> I first choose a simple, compact form which I start to deconstruct and decompose into several fragments. Through this process I am given a multiplicity of shapes, intermediate spaces and interactions. The objects are constructed with a porcelain body which is transparent. It is a very thin structure, at the limit of being easily broken. Here and there are the first signs of a crack . . .
>
> Shape, space and light don't really have a fixed reality because visually each object is constantly on the verge of losing its own balance. Any new position would provoke a different perspective of shape, space and light.

Since then Annen's sculpture has been an improvisation on this basic conical form. By changing the properties through deconstruction he can explore in depth the underlying concerns of volume, light and the interaction of space both between and inside the forms. There are obvious references to the kind of shapes and shell-like surfaces we associate with molluscs, but also to space travel through the forms of rockets and spaceships. The time scale of millennia between the earliest creatures to inhabit our planet and the shapes of technology that will ultimately transport us to other planets is also implicit in his sculpture. In this sense it is timeless.

All Annen's work comes from throwing. The basic conical form is thrown in sections which are joined together and cast in plaster in several segments. He mixes porcelain clay with tiny balls of styrofoam which will burn out during the firing but make the structure strong like bone. The clay is kept at the consistency of mud and

pressed in handfuls against the mould to a thickness of 3 cm (1⅛ in.). Wedge-shaped pieces of charcoal (which Annen burns himself in a saggar) are pushed into the soft clay. These will burn out during firing to form the holes. The sections are joined together with slip straight onto the kiln shelf and trolley so that it can be wheeled into the kiln. After the first firing of 1250°C (2282°F) a coat of porcelain slip is applied by brush and then re-fired to the same temperature so that the resulting surface cracks obscure the pitted porcelain underneath.

The bowls are basically a parabolic arch which will fire upside down without collapse. Annen uses Limoges porcelain for its qualities of translucency which is slipcast using a stopwatch set at 50 seconds. After pouring out the slip he pours in a mixture of water and deflocculent to ensure the slip thickness is completely even. This is quickly syringed out. There are two approaches to decorating: the first is to apply latex by syringe in free diagonal lines and curves followed by brushed slip. This is repeated several times before the latex is peeled away giving subtle layers of thickness. The second is to dry the newly-cast

bowl with a gas burner for three to four seconds, then to use a more powerful burner to encourage little pieces to blow away. Both techniques are instinctive and contrast with the methodical precision of his making stages. Bowls are fired inverted resting in 'sitters' (to avoid distortion) to 1250°C (2282°F) in a heavy reduction atmosphere.

Annen's life as a ceramic artist has been a search for new challenges to express his ideas and emotions. During our conversations he talked about the future, of wanting to concentrate on the qualities of whiteness and light in his work. After the interviews I spent time in the Alps, taking the train high up into the glaciers of the Eiger. Stepping out into the blinding white snow, seeing the many tonal variations of whiteness gave me an immediate rapport with where he has come from and where he is going.

Further reading

Video of Annen/Fassbaender: *Artist-in-Residence*, 'Working Process of a Large Porcelain Sculpture', Seto, Japan, 2001
Contemporary Studio Porcelain (2nd edition), Peter Lane, A & C Black, London, 2003

101

Satoru Hoshino

In ceramic work, a product of clay and fire, the work merely borrows the hand of the artist to bring out its inherent form.

SATORU HOSHINO

Portrait of Satoru Hoshino.

(Opposite) *Rain in Ancient Woodland,* 190 x 400 x 400 cm (75 x 157½ x 157½ in.), 1999.

Satoru Hoshino's career as a Japanese ceramic artist has been continually punctuated by an accolade of international awards, prizes and professorships. His work is represented in museums in Europe, Australia, America as well as Japan. Inserted into his biographical data between 'Travelled to USA' and 'Associate Professor at Canberra School of Art' is the entry for 1986 'Lost studio in landslide'. Hoshino's relationship with clay is underpinned by this traumatic experience of the earth's brute physical power. In an instant the landslide which engulfed his studio changed his conception of earth as a material he could manipulate with his hands on a human scale into a metaphor for universal energy and destruction. The very same earth which had served him as a benign artistic medium literally attacked him, revealing its nature as a phenomenon he could not control. Living in a post-industrial computerised age, it is always shocking to be confronted with the forces of nature, such as earthquake or hurricane, which still cannot be constrained by man. At such times we are reminded that earth possesses a force which as well as nurturing and supporting us can also destroy and cause chaos. This conflict is at the core of Hoshino's black ceramic installation and action work. He says of the experience:

When a disaster occurs and a person is thrown out into chaos, he makes himself into a centre and creates a passage through the chaos. To deepen relationships, find meaning, and build new order. A sudden catastrophe. A fact which cannot conceivably be removed from the world. Disaster exists just as certainly as the coming of death. Is it impossible to conceive of an order that contains such a possibility? People attempt to find words to describe the indescribable, death or disaster, and to try to under-

stand. However, there are facts that slip from the edges of the words. People try to construct order while the chaos of the universe keeps on endlessly undermining it. It is an endless struggle, but it is necessary to keep on constructing a passage.

Hoshino's early work during the 1970s and early to mid-1980s was in the style of Japanese minimalism, expressed through geometrical form and restraint. It explored such dualistic concepts as delicate/turbulent or surface/depth. Some of his investigations centred around variations of a clay block whose surface is smooth and broken up with wave patterns generating a two-dimensional image. The eye is led to the ends of the block where its edges abruptly change into its sides. Here the surface is turbulent, marked

with fingers pressing randomly into the soft clay – this 'freer' treatment expressing a precursor to his later work. Since the late 1980s Hoshino's forms have become amorphous, their surface a powerful physical evidence of his dialogue with clay as material. His work is a kind of ceramic stream of consciousness, changing form and accelerating as it flows along. He talks about his work:

My working methods are based on an expansive view of clay as basic matter, or nature, rather than just an art or craft material. I engage in a dialogue with the clay as it sits in front of me, as a soft, flexible lump of matter. This dialogue is carried out through a form of body language: the primitive action of pressing parts of my body (my fingers)

Stand on Plain, Out of Forest, 180 x 50 x 50 cm
(71 x 19¾ x 19¾ in.), 1997.

(Opposite above) *Ancient Woodland VII,* 1998.
(Opposite below) *Pein Carnate/Pre-Copernican Mud II,* 1998.

against the body of the clay. The clay responds by revealing its softness. This is not a relationship in which I am active and the clay is passive, even if I am the first to speak. If I express myself too abruptly, the clay form may collapse or crack and reject my requests. The clay is active too. The dialogue can only take place if I empathise with the material, adjusting myself to the time contained in the clay and the rhythms of nature. After repeated efforts, a form appears and develops into a work of art. This is the result of a joint effort, like that of two people in a three-legged race, between myself and the medium of clay. The form that appears does not draw attention to the physical properties of clay but rather brings out the inner life of the clay, the inner life found in the time that is shared by the clay and myself. Therefore, it should give the viewer a sensory experience, like

touching the skin, that goes beyond the sense of vision.

If an artist takes a domineering approach to the medium, forcing his desires and human concepts on it rather than engaging in a dialogue with it, he is violating the material. Some ceramic art is gaudily coloured, killing the life of the clay, and it serves only as an object of pleasure. Some ceramicists fail to bring out the individuality of the clay, forcing it into a mould as if it were plastic to produce expressionless utilitarian objects. This sort of work lacks the joy of dialogue and there is no exchange

between the artist and the work, no attempt to live and enhance the life of the clay.

In such a situation there is nothing but desire and its shadow, an unconscious sense of sin. Contemporary people experience a vague feeling of anxiety that first emerged when human beings stopped living in harmony with nature and began rearranging and attempting to control it. Energy is expended on excessive production/consumption in order to overcome this anxiety, so contemporary life leads to greater fatigue, wearing down the senses and the heart.

On the other hand, there are people in the world of ceramics who believe that ceramicists should only make vessels that are useful in everyday life, and certainly there are some ceramic objects that are nothing but embodiments of excessive desire. However, since ancient times, there have always been ritual objects and figures made of clay that are involved in the life of the spirit and employed in praying and giving thanks to the gods. I believe that we need objects that speak to the human spirit today, contemporary totems, in order to restore a symbiotic relationship with the world where human beings can live and let other forms of life live in a harmonious relationship with nature. This is the task that I see needs to be done.

It is a necessary path to the restoration of a proper kind of life. We should not use natural things as if they are physical objects. We need to re-examine our relationship with matter. Matter once taught us how to live in harmony with nature in the process of making art. Each material contains a cosmos and a possibility of an interchange between matter and human beings that nurtures the human spirit. This is the spirit that gave birth to culture. Clay is part of the earth, the mother of all life and death and the great cycle in which they move.

I would like my work to be a new form of life (a new cosmos) emerging from a sea of mud (chaos) that spreads out horizontally. I am not interested in forms assembled in the head beforehand but in forms that grow out of the vibration between the clay and my own body. I am looking for a harmonious world that appears as I listen to the time generated by the material and adjust the rhythm of the body to it. This

process also involves the overlapping of individual time with the time of the universe, extending from the distant past to the present and the future. The image that emerges out of this process should allude to the abundance of nature and have continuity with the wonderful time of ancient forests. It should be an image of the earth from whence it came.

My purpose in my current work is to rethink this relationship with matter or nature on the level of the physical body. It also extends to an exploration of the internal truth to be found in things. This work is a tentative answer to the question 'What can be done in ceramics now?'

Most of Hoshino's work has been built with coarse red earthenware clay which is black-fired in the traditional Japanese way. The forms are built up with thick 10 cm (4 in.) coils which are then manipulated, squeezed and pressed with the fingers. The pieces are fired up to around

850°C (1562°F), and as the temperature drops to 500°C (932°F) pine needles are introduced and the kiln sealed.

Since 1998, when Hoshino was guest artist at the European Ceramic Work Centre in the Netherlands, he has also been using a mixed black stoneware clay which he fires in an oxidising atmosphere to between 1150°C and 1235°C (2102°F–2255°F). This gives the large-scale work more strength.

When a piece finally emerges from the kiln, one is always surprised at the result. Sometimes it is much better than expected, or it may be quite different from anything one had imagined, taking on a life of its own. This is the moment when the unknown factor of nature intervenes in the here and now.

Further reading

'Between Order and Chaos', Tani Arata, *Ceramics: Art and Perception*, no. 15

'Pre-Copernican Mud Reincarnate', Satoru Hoshino and Tani Arata, *Ceramics: Art and Perception*, no. 39

Making sequence
(Far left) Building up the form with thick coils of soft clay which are squeezed and pressed with the fingers.
(Left) The pieces are wheeled into a trolley kiln to be fired between 1150°C and 1235°C (2102°F–2255°F).

107

Alison Gautrey

Alison Gautrey in her studio.
Photograph by Jane Perryman.

(Opposite) *Spun Porcelain Bowls,* 12 x 26 cm,
14 x 16 cm, 8 x 9 cm (4¾ x 10¼ / 5½ x 6¼ /3¼ x 3½ in.), 1998.
Photograph by Graham Murrell.

Physical movement has always been an important part of Alison Gautrey's life; her early training was to be a dancer and in her late adolescence she was teaching jazz ballet in a dance school. Injuries prevented her from pursuing this career, but she has managed to retain and transform the qualities of dance into another medium. The essence of her ceramics is to capture the feeling of movement within a simple form. It is a known fact that limitation can release creativity and Gautrey's present circumstances certainly restrict many possibilities for her work. She is the mother of three small children and has, by necessity, developed a way to splice the family demands with short bursts in the studio. Like a spinning dancer, she uses centrifugal force to spin her wafer-thin porcelain bowls. Their round bottoms emphasise the sense of movement by literally rocking and wobbling. They sit slightly off centre as they are forced to tilt slightly in order to find their centre of gravity. She says:

> The technique means everything is fluid so the form needs to be fluid too.

Gautrey grew up on a fruit farm in Cottenham near Cambridge and has returned there to set up her home and studio. She studied ceramics at Buckingham College of Higher Education in the early 1980s where she developed an innovative alternative to the traditional technique of slipcasting. She says:

> College was an amazing time to push the boundaries.

Through the search for a contemporary application to industrial techniques she came up with the idea of spinning the mould whilst casting. With the help of Harry Fraser and technicians at the Wedgwood factory she investigated ways to make it work. It took three and a half years of trial and error to resolve the problems but the success resulted in her being launched as a young designer by Rosenthal who gave her an exhibition after the degree show.

Gautrey could easily have been headhunted by industry but she remembers the 1980s as a time when

Black Stripe Spun Porcelain Bowl, 12 x 26 cm (4¾ x 10¼ in.), 1998. Photograph by Graham Murrell.

(Opposite above) *Plain Disc Spun Porcelain Bowl,* 12 x 26 cm (4¾ x 10¼ in.), 1998. Photograph by Graham Murrell.
(Opposite below) *Grey Random Line Spun Porcelain Bowls,* 12 x 26 cm (4¾ x 10¼ in.), 14 x 16 cm (5½ x 6¼ in.),
8 x 9 cm (3¼ x 3½ in.), 2000. Photograph by Marc Burden.

industry was not employing young graduates. After leaving college, and before starting her family, Gautrey combined teaching on various Arts Foundation courses with developing her technique and designs. She says:

> My work is not to do with art. It fits into the designer/retail niche.

She has realised this ambition successfully, designing for the Conran Collection and selling her work in galleries world-wide.

The idea of ceramics as an extension of the maker, in which no disguise is possible is a familiar one and very true. Gautrey's work manages to combine the sophisticated purity and detachment of translucent porcelain with something intimate and domestic. Slipcasting is an industrial process, but her bowl forms do retain a connection with the hands that made them and also to the place they were made in. Watching her at work in her studio is impressive and illuminating. She works in a converted coal bunker next to the large farmhouse kitchen – it is a long thin space and the wheel where she produces her work is at the far end surrounded by piles of white porcelain trimmings. Its location as studio is at the hub of the household and enables Gautrey to juggle her two roles of mother and ceramicist efficiently and economically. If the spun bowls were produced in a sterile environment away from the chaos of family life, they would have a completely different feel.

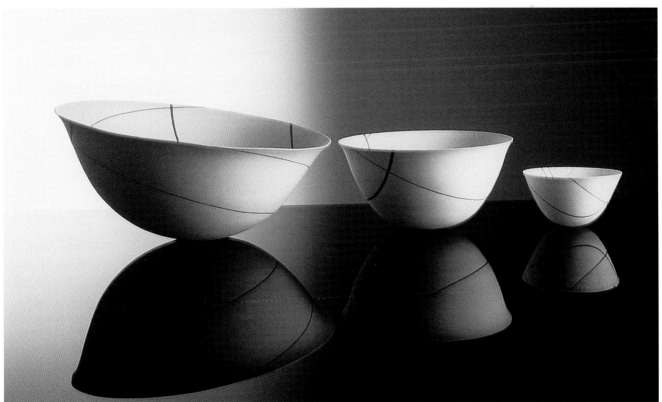

She says, 'The process does the work for you.' Gautrey's technique combines jiggering and casting. The original prototype form is turned on a whirler and cast to make a plaster mould. This mould fits into a jigger-head and, whilst revolving, the linear designs are applied first by slip trailing. Everything happens very quickly; as she compresses the slip trailer and aims it at the spinning plaster mould a rhythmic line is instantly created. At this stage Gautrey can make variations in the designs through colour and by subtle changes in the movement of her hand. Next an eggcupful of porcelain slip is poured in. The centrifugal force disperses the slip evenly all over the mould within a few seconds. Some of the surface patterns are made with bone china which has

a different shrinkage rate causing a slight dunting effect. The bowls are fired inverted on industrial sitters to avoid warping and then the edges are rubbed smooth with diamond stone.

Gautrey is at the point where she wants her work to move on. Once her children are all at school she hopes to have time to develop some of her ideas.

Further reading

Sasha Wardell, *Slipcasting*, A&C Black, 1997

Making sequence
(Above left) A linear design is applied with the slip trailer whilst the plaster mould is rotating.
(Above right) Porcelain slip is poured in; the centrifugal force immediately dispersing the slip evenly all over the mould.

Photographs by Jane Perryman.

Philippe Barde

The Swiss ceramicist Philippe Barde has the reputation of an outsider living on the edge of convention; it is a romantic and brave way to live. The location of his studio represents a fitting paradox for the production of his work and ideas. He rents the ground floor of a small two-storeyed building which used to be a bakery in the heart of Geneva. It is dwarfed and surrounded by eight storied modern apartment buildings which are squatted in by the city's youth. It has the atmosphere of the bohemian hippie era of the 1960s, with people hanging out and playing guitars; the detritus of communal living in evidence everywhere. Inside Barde's studio however is an immaculate white minimal space (divided by a bamboo blind) with a few shelves, a table, a bed, a woodstove and a kiln. A book on Morandi lies on the shelf. Barde's ceramics is cerebral and conceptual, underpinned by ambiguity and occasionally absurdity. Its essence lies in the risk of taking an idea to the limits of its possibilities through the limitations of ceramic as material.

Barde talks of himself as an obsessive traveller, collecting impressions and contacts from all over the globe. His heritage as an internationalist can easily be traced to his background; he was conceived in Vietnam and grew up in Montreal and Paris. His father was an engineer of dams and this filters through into Barde's approach to ceramics – his way of working is mathematical and sequential rather than intuitive. Barde's training began with a year at the University of Macon studying glass, followed by four years (1974–78) at the Applied Arts School in Geneva where he learnt the rudiments of earthenware, stoneware and porcelain. He was fortunate to be there at a time when Philippe Lambercy was head of ceramics; an enlightened man, influenced by the Steiner philosophy, who promoted a climate of openness through holistic investigation and discovery. Barde remembers a Japanese ceramicist called Setsako Nagasawa coming to the college to talk about naked clay. The directness of clay without glaze had a powerful effect on him to the extent that he has never used colour or glaze since. He says:

> With naked clay you can see the process – with glaze you will hide what is going on.

Philippe Barde in his studio.
Photograph by Jane Perryman.

Since then Barde's international profile has risen consistently as someone who can push boundaries and challenge our perceptions about ceramics. He has won many prizes including first prize at the Fletcher Challenge in New Zealand in 1997 and the silver prize in 2001 at the First World Ceramic Biennale in Korea. The early post-art-school years were spent exploring and experimenting with the alchemy of clay and firing. Barde describes the period as an apprenticeship to learn the language of ceramic art. He says:

> Ceramics is like Latin or Greek – it gives you a basic skill/vocabulary for life. Every generation has to change something to keep it alive. We have to make something new, we have to make a challenge. When you learn ceramics it's so difficult – so it enables you to change it into another situation.

He needed to master all the idiosyncrasies and complexities of the material before he was ready to use it as a vehicle for his ideas. He illustrates this pivotal point in time when someone has mastered their technique by paraphrasing the Swiss-German writer Ludwig Hohl:

> To learn the craft is to forget it.

(Above) *Inside and Outside Shape,* installation of 55 elements, 25/20 cm (9¾ /8 in.) each, 2001.

Photograph by Ilmari Kakinen.

(Opposite page) *Inside Shape,* installation of 20 elements, 25/20 cm (9¾ /8 in.), 2001.

In 1993 he spent time at the European Keramisch Werkcentrum in the Netherlands where his concerns revolved around an exploration of gravity by taking a form to the edge of its balance. Two black smoke-fired hemispherical bowls sit on either side of an angle-iron plinth at the point of falling off. It is a simple idea but clever in its power to engage the onlooker – our instinct is to run forward and grab it to save it from falling. Implicit is the kind of humour which resonates with slapstick comedy and clowning, but also an opposite emotional response to do with anxiety and danger. Barde works with an idea for several years, improvising on the theme and developing different solutions. Much of his work is site specific and could be classified as installation. One development here was to present a group of seven bowls, each one occupying a separate wooden plinth; some sitting 'comfortably' and 'properly' on a horizontal top and others sitting on the edge of a dramatically sloping surface. There are references to surrealism and the 'cliff-hanger' syndrome; seen in a group the message is dynamic and powerful, on the verge of containing a tangible narrative. Barde talks about 'feeling the story of the forms'.

During the mid-1990s and into the early part of this century Barde's living environment of the mountainous, pine-forested region of the Jura informed his work. By selecting a rock from which he made a plaster mould he was able to explore its qualities through repeated slipcasting and deconstruction. With each slipcasting (in porcelain) he took away a different side or facet of the rock to create an unfamiliar volume inside. Each new casting reveals a completely different aspect and gives us a fresh perspective. Barde presents us with the ambiguity of opposites; of looking not only inside the dense solid volume of rock but also right through the translucent porcelain walls into the smooth white interior. There are the underlying emotions of tension and risk by associating these two materials together; the fragile breakability of porcelain contrasting with the permanent dependability and density of rock. Another improvisation on this theme was to take the original cast of a rock and to cast the inside of it; then to cast the inside of that and so on, each casting diminishing in size until he ended up with a tiny fragment – 'the soul of the rock'.

(Above) *All the Same, All Different,* installation of 9 elements, 20/20 cm (8/8 in.), 1999.
Photograph by Jeran Philippe Geiser.

(Opposite above) *All the Same, All Different,* installation of 8 elements, 85/60/30 cm (33½/23½/11¾ in.), 1999.
Photograph by Jeran Philippe Geiser.
(Opposite below) *Seto People, Human Bowls,* dia: 30/20/15 cm (11¾/8/6 in.), 2002.
Photograph by Hayashi Tatsuo.

Barde's installation of ziggurat forms explored the antithesis of porcelain with its traditional qualities of thinness and translucency by presenting it as thick and dense. I have seen him demonstrating this technique at a symposium in Switzerland and it was a kind of perfor- mance in its own right. A basic cube form is constructed with slabs of plaster and the casting slip withdrawn at 5-minute intervals. The inside of the mould forms a series of steps representing a sequence of thicknesses relating to the timings. He then makes casts of these inner stepped

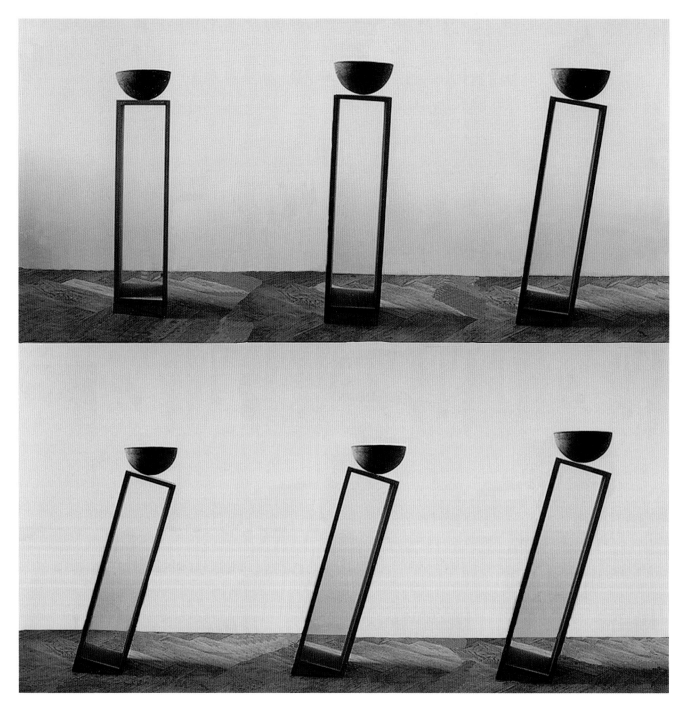

Newton 5, installation, 35 cm (13¾ in.), 1995.

forms. Their appearance is one of straightforward ziggurat at their base where the slip is thin, but each step upwards becomes more eroded and anarchic as it becomes thicker. The installation consists of groupings of the original cube castings with their stepped 'innards' and beside them their alter ego ziggurats.

Barde's work is a response to his environment and now that the rural has recently been replaced with the urban, it has given him a new direction – the subject matter around him to do with people rather than landscape. Teaching is also an important part of Barde's life; as well as a permanent part-time position at the Applied Arts School in Geneva he is regularly invited to teach in China and Japan, combining his passion for travel. On a recent trip to China, where he conducted important research into the decline of the porcelain factories at Jingdezhen, he was struck by the shape of the human face as it drinks from a tea bowl. He thought about our perception of facial beauty and how it relates to the theory of proportion in the Golden Section. He began this investigation by photographing a friend's face and translating the silhouette into a bowl form through computer graphics. He discovered that the two sides of the face are not symmetrical. A new challenge arose; how to cast a bowl with two different profiles.

Barde says that the process he uses gives him his forms – and admits that he is not skilled with form. All his work is slipcast in porcelain and fired in a range between 1250°C and 1280°C (2282°F–2336°F). For his present 'bowl portraits' he uses a metal template to make a jigger and jolley mould of the prototype forms, one of the left and one of the right contours of the face. The two solid plaster shapes representing the two profiles are cut in half and joined together, then re-cast to make a concave mould. After slipcasting, the bowl has a kind of collision line where the two unconnected halves meet. The techniques Barde uses detach him from the material of clay. It is partly this quality of detachment which allows us to respond emotionally to his message. His work has a purity about it, removed from the distractions of daily life.

The essence of Barde's work is to find an idea and express it through the very specific limitations of slipcast porcelain. He is fascinated by the narrowing down of a field of vision in order to liberate more possibilities. The paradox of freedom through restriction. He says:

The material has something philosophical and mystical about it that I work with. What I like about ceramics is that you need a deeply developed sense of observation – you need to find out what you want without asking.'

Further reading

'Philippe Barde – All Alike, All Different', Michele Baeryswil-Decloux, *Ceramics: Art and Perception*, no. 31
La Revue de la Céramique et du Verre, no. 116

Lawson Oyekan

Lawson Oyekan in his studio.
Photograph by Jane Perryman.
(Opposite) *Contiguity, Coming Up for Air,* ht: 200 cm
(79 in.), 2002.
Photograph by Paul Tucker.

There is a striking photograph of a Janus-headed pottery vessel made by the Longuda people from northern Nigeria which supplies some clues to the work of the Nigerian ceramicist Lawson Oyekan. It can be found in the ethnographer Nigel Barley's book *Smashing Pots – Feats of Clay.* The piece is made from red clay and has a bulbous, spiky body whose surface bears the energetic incision and cutting marks of a tool pressed into the soft clay. The caption reads:

> Longuda religious ritual is directed mainly towards the pacification of the spirits of disease. Small pottery images known as 'kwandalowa' are used for this purpose. In these pots the disease-producing spirits take up their abode, and diseases are transferred from the human body to the pots, which are kept in miniature huts as shrines.

Barley goes on to describe that within conscious and unconscious symbolism, 'thinking with pots' is extremely common in Africa. The potting process is a scenario which provides a concrete experience and serves as a model for organising other experiences.

The phrase 'thinking with pots' provides a graphic image of the power of raw and fired clay to permeate all areas of life in Africa, providing an instantly recognisable language and iconography. Oyekan has developed a potent spiritual and physical relationship to his material through his heritage of one of the richest pottery cultures in the world. The collective energy of this heritage has enabled his work to communicate some of the struggles of humanity and the paradoxes of the human condition. Oyekan says of his work:

> The work is a physical representation of the dynamic experience of coming up for air and is a symbol of human indestructibility, survival – and of the process of healing. Each piece is a constitution of elements that embody the rigours of survival. A kind of drama where all aspects relate to one another. The holes to the textural descriptions. The slabs to the whole

form. The light shining through the perforations to the sound of wind whistling. A drama that relates to my experience as a human being.

The pieces are self-portraits. They are derived descriptions of what it is to be human. The different elements of the pieces represent moments of experience – fragments of chaos, which I have captured and put together to form a whole, thus creating an experience of regeneration and healing. The holes represent sharp jabs of experience, yet they are windows that allow essential light and air into the very core of the piece thus dissipating the darkness, giving clarity of vision and the ability to breathe.

Seeing Oyekan's work 'in the flesh' for the first time provokes an immediate response – initially to the monumental scale and wealth of suggestive associations. It has a forceful presence which is impossible to ignore. His monolithic clay vessels tower 2–3 m (6–8 ft) high and resemble limbless torsos who announce their gender through their shape and profile. Some are vertical cylinders with enclosed tops like phallic fertility poles and some have a more female bulbous form with an opening at the top. Apart from these obvious anthropomorphic references to do with the containment of human matter and spirit, the forms also resonate with other kinds of containers. There are similar qualities to be found in the mud huts and grain containers of Africa and India, the structures built by giant termites or the mud nests built by birds to nurture their young.

One's secondary response to Oyekan's work is a desire to explore his use of surface. Upon close inspection it is obvious that the structure has been built up through the joining together of many small flat discs of clay. They remind me of the cow pats, left out to dry in the sun all over India, which bear the fingermarks of the woman who shaped them between her hands. The walls are thin for the scale of his work, giving a tension between mass and delicacy and a sense that the clay has been pushed to its limits. The surface is covered with nipplelike projections and criss-crossed with scratched lines and calligraphic signs resembling layers of graffiti on an old wall. All the markings and cuts seem to have equal importance, so the eye roves easily across the surface, never resting at one place. The rugged finish is further accentuated by regular holes and cuts which puncture right through the clay allowing the

(Below) *Contiguity, Coming Up for Air,* ht: 210 cm (83 in.), 2002.

Photograph by Paul Tucker.

(Opposite) *Contiguity, Coming Up for Air,* 2002.

Photograph by Paul Tucker.

light in and the darkness out. We are able to look in through the piercings to the soul of the piece. There is also a sense that the soul of the piece is looking out at us. In the Tribal areas of Gujarat (India), terracotta spirit houses are made by potters to house the spirits of the dead and, like Oyekan's sculptures, they also have openings – windows and doors to enable the spirits to travel in and out.

Oyekan was born in England but grew up in Nigeria where his father was a barrister and his mother a chef. He began his studies in chemistry and then spent a couple of years travelling around Europe and America to see the world, taking odd jobs to support himself. A degree as a mature student at the Central School of Art in London followed, and then graduate studies at the Royal College. Although he became a proficient thrower, Oyekan had no desire to become a production potter but began investigating ways to use clay as a vehicle for his ideas through handbuilding processes. Alison Britton, one of his tutors at the Royal College in 1990, remembers his early thrown and handbuilt work:

> I think it is the stretch of his thinking across the different forms and surfaces, rough or smooth, loose or controlled, pricked or gashed, his sensitivity to their different requirements to become themselves, that is exciting.

Oyekan talked to me about the need to discover what could be done with clay, how far he could push its boundaries and limitations, how he could use it to express his experience whilst still retaining its potency as a basic element:

> It took me many years to understand clay and feel free to work with it.

Once he had acquired this confidence Oyekan quickly found his voice and won immediate recognition after graduation during the 1990s. He describes himself as an animist and has found a way to connect his spirit to the spirit of the clay. Through his capacity to cross cultural boundaries Oyekan both excited and challenged the world of contemporary art and ceramics. The American art critic Ken Johnson describes his work as being 'sophisticatedly modern' and relating to Minimalism through the monolithic form, to Process Art through the making techniques and to the Expressionist

ceramics of Peter Voulkos through the rugged finish and scale. It is perhaps paradoxical that these modern art movements grew out of a response to non-western traditions.

At the time I met him in his temporary studio in London, he was preparing to send a piece, *Healing Being* which won the Grand Prix Award, to the First World Ceramic Biennale in Korea. Seeing a piece of Oyekan's ceramic sculpture in the sophisticated environment of a contemporary art gallery would give little indication of the many problems and obstacles surrounding its beginnings and journeys. Oyekan's struggle to find affordable studio space in London (where he lives with his partner and three small children) led him to take up a residency at a studio in Denmark where he had access to technical help and the possibility to fire work of any scale. The logistics of transporting finished work to London on a budget was solved through his old rebuilt Renault 1.6 van in which he commuted overland and by ferry between Denmark and London. He was able to fit in three sculptures at a time; two on the roof and one inside with the passenger seat removed – so the scale limitation of his pieces was determined not by the kiln but by the size of his van.

Oyekan sees his work as a series of notebooks put together to make a whole. Many of the clay slabs are incised on both sides with a significant word which could be in a variety of languages – the Yoruba word *eke* meaning hypocrisy or the German word *alles* meaning all. Enough slabs are prepared all together to build a complete piece and then stored in plastic until he is ready to start work. The sculptures are conceived and built in family groups but can also stand alone. The clay is a mixture of 50% clay, 50% grog and 8% cotton fibre (which will burn away and leave a fine network of hairline holes in the fabric of the clay). The form is built up slowly to avoid collapse, its construction method creating a structure of strength. Each section overlaps the next and is compressed together whilst the clay is soft, without the need of slip or water. The shape of the holes is made by inserting a knife and twisting it, which for Oyekan represents both his sharp jabs of experience and a passage through which the transformation of healing can occur. Many aspects of his work contain these kind of opposite elemental forces which express the inherent dichotomy of our planet (male/female; inside/outside; dark/light; gentle/aggressive; chaotic/ordered).

In the 21st century, a large percentage of the human condition is still to do with suffering and our endeavours to overcome it. Lawson Oyekan's primary concern in his work is to 'deliver a message of reassurance so that human suffering can be healed'. He has set himself a highly ambitious challenge but, as more of his work finds itself in public places and museums, it is starting to be realised.

Further reading

'The Human Presence in Clay', Alison Britton, *Ceramic Review*, no. 156

Smashing Pots – Feats of Clay from Africa, Nigel Barley, British Museum Press, 1994

'Lawson Oyekan, City Gallery, Leicester', David Jones, *Ceramic Review*, no. 153

Making sequence
(Opposite above) Building up the form with overlapping discs of clay.
(Far left) The shape of the holes is made by inserting a knife and twisting it.
(Left) The form nearing completion.

Margaret O'Rorke

Margaret O'Rorke in her studio.

Photograph by Jane Perryman.

Wall Sculpture Installation with Light, ht: 244 cm (96 in.),
w: 91 cm (35¾ in.), 1995.

Photograph by Allen Miles.

Margaret O'Rorke talks about being the vehicle of expression for her chosen material of translucent porcelain. She is concerned with 'retaining the life in the clay, the nature of the material and the adventures we have with it.' The dictionary defines 'adventure' as 'a risky undertaking of unknown outcome, an exciting or unexpected event or course of events, a hazardous financial operation'. Although O'Rorke says she is not an academic or intellectual ceramicist and finds it hard to talk about her work, she has an instinct for getting things right and her choice of words here is a good example. The definition gives a pertinent description of the many highs and lows a ceramicist experiences – for within the 'adventure' of raw clay being manipulated and fired into ceramic is always its opposite – the element of disaster. Through her understanding of the material and its qualities of translucency, she is able to produce work which combines the fluidity and sensuality of thrown porcelain with the drama of man-made light.

O'Rorke's approach is not calculated; she works instinctively and her ceramics express a sense of sensuality and spontaneity. To see one of her porcelain lights as it is switched on is to experience something instantly magical, like looking up at a full moon or at the galaxy in a clear night sky. Her pieces combine the universal elements of earth, light and space with a unique approach outside the mainstream of ceramic tradition. O'Rorke has placed herself in a challenging role of making connections between clay and light within the limitations of electrical engineering. In glazed ceramics the light travels from outside to inside and is reflected off the surface. Her concern is to reverse this principle and direct the light from within and send it *beyond*. In our conversation she emphasises this word which is defined as 'the unknown; the world outside the range of man's perception'. It is the ability of the light to travel through the porcelain and radiate outwards that impassions her. Her work is both sophisticated and accessible, existing comfortably in domestic or public environments and can be classified as light sculpture.

After leaving school early at 16 years old she spent a

year at Chelsea School of Art studying painting before taking a ceramics degree at Camberwell School of Art in London. Here she was fortunate to be introduced to porcelain by Lucie Rie. Marrying early, raising a family and running a restaurant occupied O'Rorke's early years until at the age of 40 she was ready to work with clay again. She set up her first studio in 1981 producing a range of tableware and domestic pots. She describes how she began with porcelain:

> When showing a painter friend how translucent porcelain can be, I suddenly wondered why I shouldn't show the translucency by using light from within. However, like all new ideas, there were huge hurdles to overcome. I was drawn to the potter's wheel from the beginning so that my work has always grown from thrown forms. It is the concentrated energy that flows instantly and directly from the body through the hands and into the clay that I love to experience, wanting this to be readable when the work is fired and lit. Several years were spent struggling to raise thrown forms tall and thin enough to emit light and be able to contain the fitting.
>
> Potters using porcelain will know that the nature of the body does not lend itself easily to this, needing water to enable the clay to move through the hands, and that it quickly collapses when it is too wet. Slowly my understanding and skills developed as I became familiar with the materials and processes – which concentrated hard work, trial and error can bring.

O'Rorke's technical struggles with the material were overcome when she discovered the blow torch and its ability to dry clay instantly. It meant she could throw her forms all in one and avoid collapse by force drying them. Having been trained as a vessel maker there were many problems of adapting electrical fittings to her pieces. However, her father had been an engineer and this heritage gave her the confidence to accept the challenge of working with electricity and the paraphernalia of wiring and light fittings.

> A visit to Lucie Rie was encouraging. Nervously plugging in one of my pieces by her fireplace I asked, 'Do you think it is all right to introduce electric light in

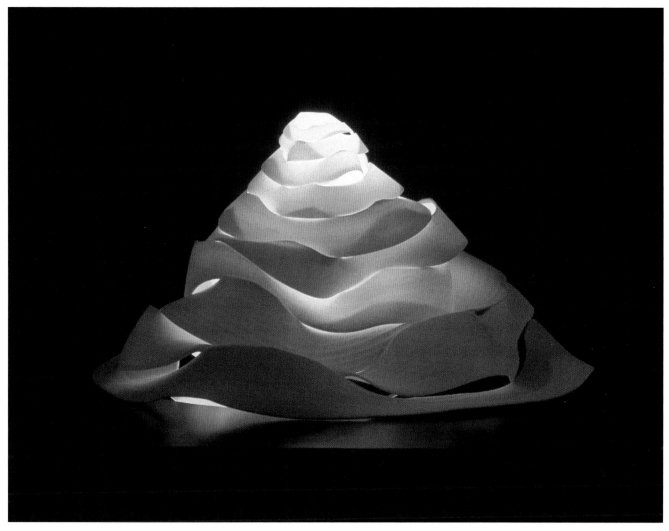

(Above) Thrown rings cut, joined and reformed during firing, ht: 20 cm (8 in.), dia: 38 cm (15 in.), 1995.
Photograph by Arnold Borgerth.

(Opposite) Thrown *Pod* suspended from 12-volt track system, ht: 16 cm (6¼ in.), dia: 16 cm (6¼ in.), 1998.
Photograph by Sebastian Hedgco.

a pot?' Her reply 'Why not?', confirmed my determination to pursue this path of thrown translucent porcelain forms giving light.

An important turning-point came in O'Rorke's development when she was invited to spend three months in the studio of the Japanese potter Ryoji Koie. She had hosted him in 1991 when he was a guest at the International Potters' Festival at Aberystwyth and he wanted to return her hospitality. She remembers the experience:

When I saw what crazy things Koie did with the clay I thought I could do it too. I couldn't work with the clay he gave me – the clay wouldn't go up. It was a crisis – I could only throw tiny things which I had to build up. It was hot and humid and there was no-one who spoke English. So I had to devise ways – I started to carve the clay. Now when I look at that work it's the most exciting I've ever done. My philosophy was not to expect anything, but to see what I could find there. Because of this, the hardship and difficulties didn't affect me as much as the other westerners there.

Cast Ceiling Light, dia: 47 cm (18½ in.).
Photograph by Colin Hall.

Returning to England, O'Rorke's work began to loosen up; instead of trying to control the material as she had done before, she began to take more risks and to trust her intuitive response. It is well known that people cannot move forward until they are ready. Within a remarkably short time she had absorbed the essence of Koie's philosophy – discarding a quest for perfection for the expression of freedom and lightness of spirit. She had found her voice artistically and literally and was taken up as a regular exhibitor by Galerie Besson in London. Large-scale commissions for site-specific work followed, enabling her to explore scale and the element of water through fountain design. She says:

Scientific knowledge can resolve many technical questions, but amid the vast arena of historical awareness and technical information potters today have to find their own creative language which can reflect, connect with and contribute to other people's feeling within our time. This is the aspect of being a potter of which I am increasingly conscious. To find a way of capturing and communicating what we feel with clay and allow the fire to transform this immediate soft, close experience into something permanent and translucent, captures my imagination and cannot be fully transmitted into words.

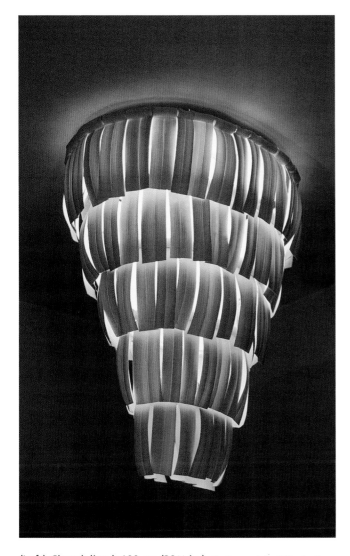 

(Left) *Chandelier*, l: 100 cm (39½ in.). Photograph by Gilles Le Corre.
(Right) *Wall Light Sculpture,* ht: 23 cm (9 in.), l: 90 cm (35½ in.). Photograph by Allen Miles.

O'Rorke's work has developed through trial and error and technical advice from friends such as Joanna Constantinidis and Sebastian Blackie. She says:

> I never would read a book. My tools were always made from packing case wire and clock springs.

An idea is originally realised in her sketchbook, then she plays around with the clay, observing how it moves and the kind of forms that appear. A consultation with the lighting engineer leads to the compromise of a solution. An important percentage of the creativity is related to the engineering, and it is this limitation which gives her work

its edge. Forms are thrown on the hump from Audrey Blackman porcelain, then a blow torch is used to firm the clay walls sufficiently to be able to cut and handle them. It also helps to control the moisture content so that sculptural forms can be made, reformed, joined and completed while the clay is leatherhard. Pieces are dried slowly so that each part can shrink and join evenly.

> While making I think about form, light and the space it encompasses to create a unified whole, always seeking ways of concealing the electrical fitting and source. Some sculptural forms also incorporate water which means much time experimenting to learn the

nature of yet another element and find technical solutions to combine all three within the final piece.

After the reduction firing to 1300°C (2372°F), which gives a high level of translucency, the surface retains the directness and definition of the making process. It is still alive.

O'Rorke's adventures through clay have enabled her to travel widely through exhibitions in Australia, America and Europe. These periods of time away from the workshop are important to feed O'Rorke with new impressions and experiences which contribute to the development of her work. She was particularly struck by the desert landscapes of California and Australia where plants have adapted to the harsh conditions of heat and drought. In the late 1990s she was awarded a grant to investigate creating industrially-manufactured porcelain lighting for domestic and large-scale installations. She spent three months working in Wades Ceramics Ltd, a factory in Stoke-on-Trent where she was given access to their technical, mouldmaking and production team. She developed a viable design with the expertise of Beverly Bingham, a lighting technologist who continues to assist her with her studio work.

Margaret O'Rorke uses a quote by Seamus Heaney as an insight into that elusive state an artist of any medium is striving for:

> As artists there's a lot of me, me, me; it's all a struggle. Just occasionally the results of me, me, me float off and become an it. It's only through working that it can happen.

This state has been described by artists of all mediums throughout history. O'Rorke has arrived at a place where she can forget herself and allow the clay to sing.

Further reading

Ceramic Technology for Potters and Sculptors, Yvonne Hutchinson Cuff, University of Pennsylvania Press, 1996

'Light Work', Margaret O'Rorke, *Ceramic Review*, no. 175

Porcelain, Caroline Whyman, Batsford, 1995

'Porcelain Light Sculptures', Margaret O'Rorke, *Ceramics: Art and Perception* no. 29

Sandra Black

Sandra Black is an Australian ceramicist internationally known for her investigations into carved and pierced porcelain vessels. She has developed a distinctive personal style expressing her ideas through symmetrical decoration on both thrown and slipcast forms. She says of her work:

The pierced vessels were inspired by the work of Angela Vardon and also my interest in corals and the drawings of Ernst Haeckel, a German biologist. The technique of piercing is particularly challenging, a process that is about both light transmission and positive and negative shapes. Recent forms have introduced elements of geometry and are kept very simple to carry the elaborate patterning.

Black uses both slipcast porcelain and bone china as well as thrown porcelain for her pierced work. The piercing takes place at the leatherhard stage with a small electric drill, taking care to choose a time when the clay is neither too damp – nor too dry. Once the surface is dry it is sanded smooth and fired to the appropriate temperature – often placed on the rim to avoid distortion. After firing, the piece is soaked in water to eliminate dust, and polished with Wet and Dry sandpaper.

Triangular Pierced Vessel, ht: 6.5 cm (2½ in.), w: 18 cm (7 in.), 2001. Photograph by Victor France.

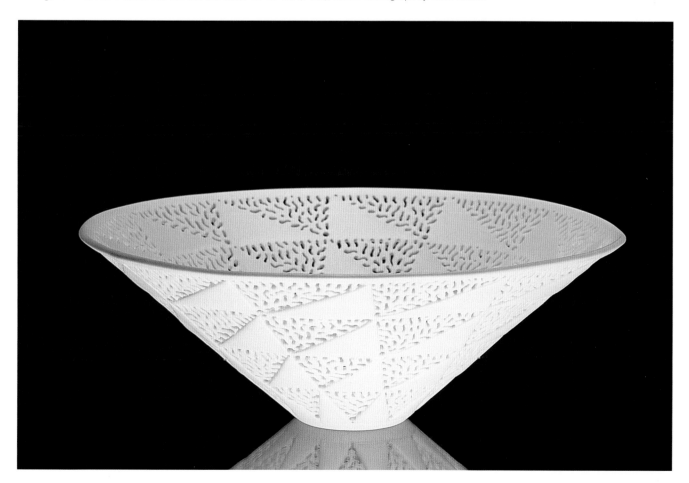

Fleur Schell

F leur Schell lives and works in Western Australia where she investigates porcelain and china clay as media for sound sculptures. Instead of utilising the translucent qualities associated with these clays, she exploits their ringing and singing properties. She says of her work:

My porcelain-based work has several unique characteristics; it incorporates recycled mixed media of diverse origins, encourages the audience to interact with it through its moving parts and often produces sound. The incorporation of found objects reflects my love for the history and layered landscape of the family farm, and the diversity of discarded building materials and obsolete machinery scattered across the landscape. The use of sound originates from my passion for music and I also occasionally apply raised braille quotes to the surface to invite a tactile experience.

Schell uses combinations of slipcasting, throwing and handbuilding for her pieces, using porcelain which is mixed with paper (paper clay) for joining thrown and slipcast sections. Firing is to 1260°C (2300°F).

A Touch Preserved, (wood, wire & porcelain), 30 x 20 cm (11¾ x 8 in.), 2001. Photograph by Robert Frith.

David Jones and Jane Perryman

High-fired porcelain vessels by David Jones, (1300°C/2372°F, polished with diapads).
Photograph by Rod Dorling.
(See chapter 2, p.94–5, for an explanation of his work.)

(Left) Burnished Vessel by Jane Perryman.
Photograph by Graham Murrell.
(See chapter 2, pp.79–83, for an explanation of her work.)

Clay with Additions

The ceramicists in this section mix a variety of additions to their clay bodies in order to achieve colour and texture in their work. The additives include oxides, combustible materials and aggregates which are dispersed evenly through the material producing qualities of depth. A shared concern with the clay itself and a desire to allow it to express its particular qualities underpins the work of these makers. Violette Fassbaender, Jeanne Opgenhaffen and Jennifer Lee are all inspired by landscape and its subtle associations. Lee's timeless vessels are built from bands and haloes of muted coloured clays with references to arid landscapes and eroded natural forms. Opgenhaffen's murals are built from tiny coloured porcelain tiles which resonate with the changing coloration of rock strata. Fassbaender expresses the qualities of bare rock and glaciers in her sculptural forms through the application of thin sheets of coloured and dried clays to her surfaces.

The roots of Thomas Hoadley and Dorothy Feibleman's work can be found in the Japanese technique of neriage. Hoadley allows the painstakingly arduous preparation of mixing and layering clays to appear effortless through his adoption of a fluid approach to handbuilding his bowl forms. Felicity Aylieff has pioneered the addition of aggregates to the clay body, producing ambiguous sculpture which unites the seductive tactile surface with a cooler more detached form. Sasha Wardell has adapted industrial techniques to produce her translucent bone china bowls which reveal internal layers of colour where the clay wall is sliced. Claudi Casanovas expresses the essence and energy of clay on the edge of destruction in his sculpture. He uses innovative techniques of mixing different clays with combustible materials to form a 'block', then freezing and dropping it to encourage fissures and cracks to appear.

(Opposite) *Vessel*, Thomas Hoadley, 15 x 17.5 x 17cm (6 x 6⅞ x 6¾in.).

Jennifer Lee

Portrait of Jennifer Lee in her studio.
Photograph by Jane Perryman.

(Opposite) (Left) *Speckled Coral Pot, Haloed Bands*,
ht: 8.7 cm (3¼ in.), w: 16 cm (6¼ in.), 2003.
(Right) *Dark Pot, Sand Band, Tilted Rim*,
ht: 28.6 cm (11¼ in.), w: 14 cm (5½ in.), 2003.
Photograph by Michael Harvey.

Lee's creations touch the spirit because ultimately they are collaborations – with earth, gravity, time and motion.

LEAH OLLMAN, *Los Angeles Times*

Watching Jennifer Lee applying a coil to an open bowl form in her London studio transported me momentarily to the traditional coil builders of India. Because of the caste system, the skill of Indian potters has evolved from generations of potters before them, equipping them with an instinctive economy of movement. Anthropologists describe this as 'ancestral knowledge'. I have rarely seen an equivalent in western potters, but that day I glimpsed it in the work of Jennifer Lee. She comes from a farming family in Aberdeenshire and although she refutes direct references in her work, her heritage firmly links her to the earth and her chosen material.

Lee's perfectly balanced pots have an elemental, pared-down quality like a skeleton removed of flesh, their strong presence speaking of timelessness. This concept of time can be seen in her work on several levels, both in the past and in the present. The history of each piece contains both the concentrated energy of her previous work and the meticulous research she undertakes before each new beginning. It contains intense handling time through repetitive building and refining over several weeks in order to produce a finished form. Like all ceramicists, Lee's work literally turns geological time around. The clay she uses has been softened into its plastic state through geological change, and by her addition of natural oxides and the firing process, she brings the vessels back to their beginnings as stone. They convey a potent resonance with the essence of rocks, pebbles, stone and sand in their colours, forms, and tactile qualities.

Her vessel forms are coiled from clays coloured with oxides so that the speckles, bands and haloes of colour run through the inner and outer walls, the colours and shapes continually changing as you move around the piece. Lee is not interested in direct references to the natural world, but rather through association. 'I find it

dangerous to look for roots – things filter through.' She talks about her pots being about 'the specific and closely observed', and there is much evidence of this in her studio. There are collections of bones, shells and seed pods systematically stored in drawers as a naturalist would do. A line of eucalyptus leaves brought back from distant travels are pinned to the wall, sequenced so that the curve of each one gradually increases from almost vertical to a crescent moon shape.

Lee's concerns also touch upon the effect of time on the world around us; of decay, corrosion and erosion; of the way colours and textures start to bleed and trans-migrate from one to another. The qualities of rusting metal, decrepit walls, ageing wood and rock are absorbed into her work and although these concerns are with impermanence, the firing paradoxically brings her work back to a permanent state. She quotes the film-maker Andrei Tarkovsky from his book *Sculpting in Time*:

> It is a mistake to talk of the artist 'looking for' his subject. In fact the subject grows within him like a fruit and begins to demand expression.

Lee studied ceramics and tapestry under Tony Franks at Edinburgh School of Art where Mick Brettle, one of her tutors, introduced her to coloured clay. This was followed by a period of travel to the west coast of North America where she visited the ceramicists Voulkos and Soldner and experienced the impact of desert landscape for the first time. Her introduction to prehistoric American Indian culture led her to make it the subject of her thesis whilst studying for her MA at the Royal College of Art in the early 1980s. A Crafts Council setting-up grant enabled her to set up a studio at 401½ where she worked for four years before moving into her present house and studio in Camberwell, London. Initially Lee interspersed some teaching with making, but for the last 10 years has been working solely as a maker. Lee's profile has consistently risen to the point where she exhibits regularly in some of the best ceramics galleries in Europe, America and Japan, and has work in many major museums and collections. Exhibiting abroad gives her the opportunity to travel which she finds important to extend and reinforce visual experience.

The progression of Jennifer Lee's work has been gradual, a systematic exploration of the inner and outer

volumes and spaces of the vessel. The open bowl forms invite the eye to move continually from inner to outer surfaces setting up a dynamic between the bands of colour and texture against the strong definition of the rim. The taller forms springing up from their narrow bases are fluid, their balanced asymmetry and slightly indented waists giving them the poise of a dancer. All her work is handbuilt with coloured clay using traditional pinching and coiling techniques. The clay body is T-Material which is mixed with natural oxide pigments

(Above) *Speckled Pot, Haloed Granite Band, Olive Rim,* ht: 17.4 cm (6¾ in.), w: 28.8 cm (4½ in.). Photograph by Michael Harvey.

(Opposite) *Pale Pot, Speckled Rim,* ht: 20.8 cm (8¼ in.), w: 11.5 cm (4½ in.), 1997. Photograph by Michael Harvey.

(between 0.25% and 4%) using Brongniart's Formula (see p.143) so that colours can be duplicated at a later date. The oxides are ground in a pestle and mortar, then added to her slaked-down clay. The coloured clay is then dried out on plaster bats, wedged and bagged ready to use. Test tiles are made from every colour batch, labelled and

fired in an oxidation atmosphere. She describes the making process:

Before I begin building, the batches of clay to be used are determined. Colour decisions are made with reference to test tiles. By referring to sketches and

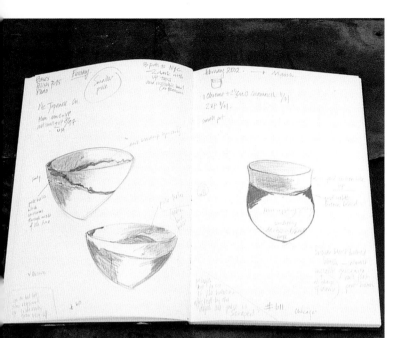

(Left) Jennifer Lee's sketchbook.

Making sequence
(Below left) A flattened coil is added to the rim of a bowl.
(Below right) Burnishing with agates to smooth and
compress the surface.

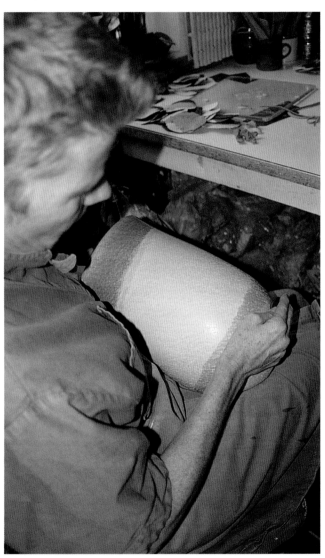

drawings from previous pieces the pot evolves and it continues to develop during the making process. The base is pinched and left to firm. The remainder of the pot is constructed with coils, some flattened to produce wide strips and added to sections. Bands are smoothed using bamboo and wooden tools. After completing the rim the pot is left until firm enough to scrape with metal kidneys to give an

even thickness. The pot is then burnished with agates to smooth and compact the clay. I spend between one and three weeks on each piece. For the last eight years the majority of my work has been fired in an electric kiln – oxidation atmosphere – to Orton cone 8 or 9. I fire slowly to 1230°C (2246°F) and soak the kiln for 1–2 hours allowing the coloured clay to mature. After firing, pots are

Olive Pot, Haloed Stone band, Coned Rim, ht: 19.6 cm (7¾ in.), w: 11.6 cm (4½ in.). Photograph by David Cripps.

worked on with emery paper and glass grinding materials to refine and polish the surfaces.

The scientific experimentation and recording of pigmentation and firing means that Jennifer Lee can plan precisely the interaction and composition of colours within the forms. She has said:

> I'm very meticulous. I admire the chemist's attitude; experimentation, exploring new materials, the precision of measuring and systematically recording results.

Instead of drawing her pots before she begins making, Lee draws them after the firing so that any unpredictable result can be preserved. But with ceramics, we never have complete control and it is this element of uncertainty, of the unknown, which gives her work its edge and tension.

Note
Brongniart's formula: $w = \dfrac{p \times g}{g - 1}$

(Where w = dry content of 1 pint slip
p = weight of 1 pint slip
g = relative density of dry clay)

Further reading

Review of exhibition at Frank Lloyd Gallery, Leah Ollman, *Los Angeles Times*, 3rd May, 2002

'The Anatomy of Things', Adam Levy, *La Revue de la Céramique et du Verre*, no. 75

'Jennifer Lee, Handbuilt Ceramics', Karen Livingstone, *Neue Keramik*, May/June 1994

'Graceful, Tilting Contours of Clay' Christopher Andreae, *The Christian Science Monitor*, 8th April, 1991

Violette Fassbaender

Portrait of Violette Fassbaender in her studio.
Photograph by Jane Perryman.
(Opposite above) *Sculpture* (front view),
ht: 34 cm (13 Æ in.), l: 49 cm (19₀ in.), 2000.
(Opposite below) *Sculpture* (back view),
ht: 34 cm (13Æ), l: 49 cm (19₀ in.), 2000.

Having lived for many years close to the flat fenlands of East Anglia I understand the powerful effect of landscape on the human psyche. Whilst passing through the Alps, early travellers on the Grand Tour closed the blinds of their carriages in order to avoid the overwhelming effect of the huge mountains. During a similar journey between Brienz and Lucerne I also experienced the dramatic panorama of mountainous landscape and realised how the work of the Swiss ceramicist Violette Fassbaender has been informed by her native scenery. Her sculptural pieces resonate with the jagged bare rocks high above the tree line whose planes and crisp edges are crisscrossed with fissures. Their structure is given further definition by lustrous white sheets of snow.

Fassbaender is primarily concerned with enclosed volume expressed through the relationship between a free form and the kind of surface marking and coloration associated with rock strata. Her recent forms appear to have grown organically rather than being built in any kind of predetermined way, existing freely in time and space. She talks about the ambiguity of how to physically place her work; unlike a ceramic vessel it has no particular viewpoint and could just as easily be turned upside down or onto its side. She says:

> I like something that's not fixed – you don't look at it and its fixed – you can change it. My biggest interest is in the clay itself – I like the feeling of raw clay and want my work to express that. I am interested in structure and the rhythm of structure; the rhythm of what I do intentionally and the rhythm that nature gives you. I work with the rhythm of contrast; the rhythm of different volumes; of fullness and flatness.

Violette Fassbaender lives in the same four-storeyed townhouse she grew up in close to the medieval centre of Basel in Switzerland. Her parents were both professional musicians and as a child she was introduced to the world of visual art and architecture. At 19, a gap year took her

(Above) *Division*, ht: 30 cm (11⅞ in.), l: 60 cm (23ẑ in.), 2002.

(Opposite) *Sculpture*, ht: 53 cm (21 in.), l: 51 cm (20 in.), 2001.

on an exchange to Japan where by chance she was introduced to clay at a pottery class. An immediate rapport with the material led her to join a professional course, committing herself for a further two years and prompting her to learn Japanese. She liked the aesthetic 'feel' of Japan; the simplicity of design and the underlying Zen philosophy underpinning the ceramic tradition. It was very different to Swiss culture.

Whilst travelling around Japan at the end of her course she met the important conceptual ceramic artist Araki Takako, an open-minded and well-travelled intellectual who offered Fassbaender work as her assistant. The 'apprenticeship' lasted for over five years during which time she learnt the basic grounding of studio practice and started to develop her own work using Takako's techniques of inlaid silk screen designs. Unlike an apprentice-

ship in Switzerland where the emphasis would be on functional production ceramics, with Takako she was able to learn and explore technique in a free way. In Japan the emphasis was on how to express a concept through the material, of how to adopt ceramic techniques to a specific project.

Returning to Basel in 1986 she rented a studio and ran classes for amateur potters while developing a range of her own thrown slip-decorated stoneware teapots. Fassbaender soon found the technique of wheel throwing restrictive, resulting in work which she found to be too tight and controlled. In 1992 an invitation to do a workshop and exhibition in Germany was the catalyst to take her back into the sculptural forms she had learnt in Japan. For the next few years she investigated volume through press-moulded double-walled bowls and elliptical

forms which were burnished and black-fired (see p.93). As well as the dramatic expressiveness of high rocky mountains in her present work, Fassbaender has also been influenced by landscapes connected to water. Switzerland has many lakes and as a child she spent weekends and holidays at Lake Constance where the melancholy and silence of foggy winters remained etched in her memory. Associations with this experience were expressed through contrasting matt and shiny surfaces resembling reflections in water, and mottled surfaces marked with the saggar-fired residue of organic material. By gradually increasing the scale of these forms and using a combination of stoneware and porcelain clays she was able to achieve different intensities of black from the saggar firing. She says:

> With large work you are able to enter the blackness of the piece.

She is describing the kind of sensation we experience when standing in front of a large canvas – of being absorbed into it rather than merely observing it as an outsider.

Again feeling restricted by technique and the limitation of round forms, Fassbaender challenged herself to find a new direction and during the last few years began handbuilding with combinations of slabs and coils. This new approach to making became her 'free form' which she resolved and exhibited successfully in 2001 during an artist-in-residency programme in Seto, Japan. She replaced low-temperature fired burnishing with high temperature stoneware.

> Now the work doesn't change much in the firing. I can't make it more interesting by firing it – I have to think about the piece from the beginning.

She now uses an iron stoneware clay to build her forms in such a way that the processes of manipulated raw clay are celebrated and evident after firing. Two sides of the form are coiled with fingermarks deliberately left and the third

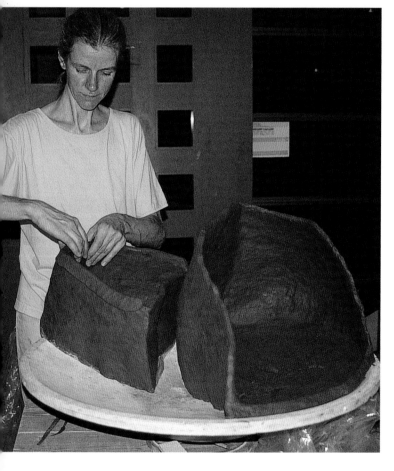

side is formed from a slab impregnated with rolled dried clays of contrasting colours and types. Some sections are covered with a thin slab of fireclay which forms a resist during the reduction firing of 1250°C (2282°F). When the fireclay is removed the contrast of red oxidised clay and dark brown reduced clay is revealed. Fassbaender's working rhythm is orientated towards exhibition deadlines but the periods of time in-between are important. This is a time for experimenting both practically by testing clays and intellectually by enjoying the cultural life of Bern through exhibitions and concerts. She maintains strong links with Japanese ceramicists and is regularly invited back to Japan for symposiums and exhibitions.

Whilst studying in Japan Fassbaender met the ceramicist Arnold Annen and for the last 10 years they have been partners, sharing a studio together where they live and work. The two large front windows of their house have been adapted into two spotlit showcases, revealing to the outside world who they are and what they do. The left window contains one of Annen's porcelain bowls; in the right is one of Fassbaender's 'free forms'. It is an interesting juxtaposition: the white translucency and weightlessness of porcelain contrasted with an enclosed voluminous free form, dark and mysterious. Both are imbued with rich associations to the Swiss landscape of rocky mountains and icy glaciers.

Further reading

Video of Fassbaender/Annen: *Artist-in-Residence*, 'Building of Multi-clay Sculpture', Seto, Japan, 2001

Making sequence
(Top left) Preparing the different clay layers; rolled into a slab.
(Left) Using combinations of slabs and coils to build the 'free form'.

Thomas Hoadley

Thomas Hoadley is considered one of the leading nerikomi artists in the United States. Nerikomi is a traditional Japanese technique of using coloured clays to create pattern blocks or loaves which are sliced into thin sections and joined together to form vessels using hand-building methods. The particular kind of skills required to master this technique can easily be traced back to his early upbringing. His father was an engineer – a profession demanding rational, systematic thinking – and his mother was artistic – involved in painting and quilt making. Through the combination of surface, form and colour with mathematical design, Hoadley's nerikomi work represents a perfect example of the equal influence of his two parents. Despite the painstaking techniques involved to produce a final piece, these open sculptural vessels celebrate the seductive plasticity of porcelain in its raw state. Their slightly undulating surfaces and rims set up a dynamic with the strong vertical emphasis of broken-up patterns and colours. It is as if in its final form the piece has a life and integrity of its own, liberated from its highly controlled beginnings to find its place in the world. Hoadley's work achieves that elusive state of effortlessness which we can see in a concert pianist or dancer. He says:

> The softness and elasticity of clay has its own intelligence – it imposes its own signature on whatever pattern I impose on the clay. My work is about a collaboration between the clay and my ideas.

Hoadley's instinct for volume and space was further developed while studying sculpture at Amherst College, Massachusetts followed by a period of working for a firm of architects. Like other ceramicists I've interviewed for this book, he discovered clay 'on the side' through recreational evening classes. This turned into a real commitment when he became an apprentice to the studio potter Malcolm Wright in Vermont (who himself had been apprenticed in Japan and was carrying on Japanese traditions using a wood-burning kiln). An MA in ceramics at Illinois university was spent concentrating on functional pottery. Hoadley describes how he discovered nerikomi:

Portrait of Thomas Hoadley outside his studio.
Photograph by Jane Perryman.

I was introduced to nerikomi while in graduate school by a Japanese potter who gave a weekend demonstration. My fascination led to a period of experimentation, but the technique was set aside while I explored other areas. A few years later, after one or two failed attempts at creating and selling a wholesale line of pottery, I was casting about for what to do next and was reminded of my earlier interest in nerikomi. About the same time, a wise bit of advice was passed on to me: I was urged to make the very best work that I could and that marketing and sales would follow.

My initial attraction to the nerikomi technique came from its organic union of pattern and structure. Rather than the former being applied to the latter, as in most decorative pottery traditions, the two are one and the same. The natural world abounds with this sort of union and, as a result, offers endless inspiration for pattern making. The other aspect that was particularly attractive to me was the translation of the

(Above) *Vessel*, 26 x 20 x 19 cm (10¼ x 8 x 7½ in.), 1999.

(Opposite) *Vessel*, 16 x 19 x 16 cm (6¼ x 7½ x 6¼ in.), 2001.

Making sequence
(Right) Preparing the clay; thin slices of grey clay have been sandwiched in between thicker slices of black porcelain. Here the loaf is opened in preparation for the third slice.
(Below right) The loaf is reassembled after the fourth slice has been added.

(Below) *Vessel*, 16 x 22 x 20 cm (6¼ x 8¾ x 8 in.), 2001.

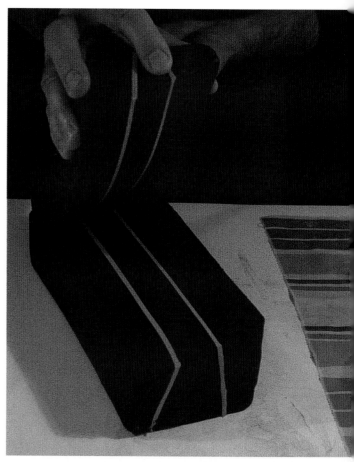

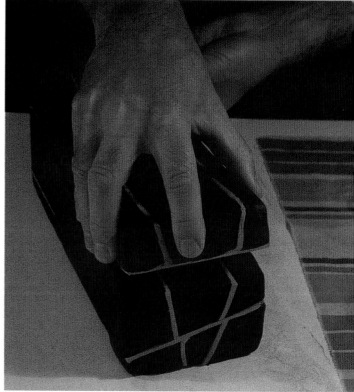

Vessel, 15 x 17.5 x 19 cm (6 x 6¾ x 7½ in.), 2000.

physical properties of clay into a visual format. By this I mean the very plasticity of the clay is made visible in the way that an imposed pattern is altered. Straight parallel lines are created by stacking up slices of variously coloured clays but in the manipulation of the resulting soft block of clay, the lines become undulating or are perhaps made to taper down to a hair's breadth. Porcelain of course shows off this quality to its greatest extent, but the principle is the same with clay. I think of my patterns as being a cooperation between my imposed structure and the clay's wise alteration of that structure.

Earlier pieces were formed from one sheet of patterned clay pressed into two-part plaster moulds taken from wheel-thrown forms. A change came about in 1987, after Hoadley took a year off to build his house in a rural wooded area of western Massachusetts. He talks of this break as being a precious, productive time for experimentation, for having the space to absorb new ideas. The single sheet of clay evolved into his distinctive patchwork technique where blocks of different patterns are combined like the patches of fabric on an Amish quilt. It is interesting that the landscape surrounding his new environment was also broken up in this way with fragments of woods interspersed with fields divided by stone walls. Gradually the limitations of using moulds led him to explore free-form shapes with the help of less restrictive drape moulds.

Hoadley mixes oxides and stains to porcelain to create his coloured clay bodies which can be read as permutations of the earth tones of New England: rich muted rusts, greys, black and white. These are sliced and stacked in various ways to create a variety of pattern blocks; some graphically complex, some illusionist and some softer and less busy. Inspiration for the designs comes from a broad source including Japanese kimonos, textiles and graphics. Cross-sectional slices from various blocks are joined to each other using slab-building techniques and added to a drape-moulded shallow bowl form which becomes the base of the vessel. The completed form is compressed, stretched, and given its final undulating shape. After carefully controlled drying the leatherhard pieces are scraped inside and out to remove the smeared clay and refine the form. When bone dry they are sanded, bisque fired to 950°C (1742°F) then wet-sanded before a second firing to 1200°C (2192°F). Finally the pieces are wet-sanded again and sealed with water seal. It is at this point that the gold leaf is applied before a coat of mineral oil which is rubbed on and washed off.

It is significant that Hoadley also paints pictures. There are obvious references in his approach to composition in his ceramic vessels with the vertical and horizontal emphasis of a two-dimensional plane. His complete integration of surface pattern and three-dimensional form means that the designs can also be seen inside the vessel. Hoadley has achieved a kind of three-dimensional 'canvas', the dialogue between inner and outer colours and designs continually vibrating and changing as we change our viewpoint. The word *nerikomi* is from the Japanese, meaning 'to mix' and 'to press into' referring to the mix of coloured clays to create patterns, and the pressing of the clay into moulds. Hoadley has taken the technique and, like all dedicated artists, over time developed it in his own unique way.

Felicity Aylieff

The flexibility of clay is limitless. Wood, slate, stone, etc. have their own virtues but compared with clay I find them restrictive. I'm driven by the desire to explore and discover new ways of using clay and I am constantly surprised by the diverse possibilities for expression in clay.

FELICITY AYLIEFF

The dichotomy of opposing forces sets up the necessary tensions and dynamics for exceptional art, whether in performance, literature, or the visual and applied arts. Felicity Aylieff's recent exploration of sculptural work has in some ways adopted qualities of detachment and distance in its departure from the traditional techniques and references of pottery making. Within its spirit however, lies the opposite of dispassion; for it is essentially seductive, exotic and female, allowing us to experience a wide range of emotions and responses. These opposites and areas of ambiguity (between ceramics and sculpture, between utility and meaning, between coolness and passion) set up a visual tension that gives the work a magnetic *gravitas*, making us not only want to approach it but caress it too. She has said:

My work is about playing with the relationships between surface and form to produce visual texture – an interdependence between tactile qualities and optical depth. This, and the internal volume, rhythm, and movement, is to elicit a more direct emotional response to the material. The material's ability to evoke positive and celebratory emotions is reflected through forms which suggest an irrepressible energy or life force.

Aylieff comes from an artistically aware background. Her father, Roy Aylieff, was an engineer involved in the manufacturing of objects and concerned with contemporary design during the 1960s and 1970s. As well as her experience of all the specific processes involved at factory floor level, she also remembers artists coming to the house to visit the family. In her formative years she learnt about a critical and

Portrait of Felicity Aylieff outside her studio.
Photograph by Jane Perryman.

Terracotta Plate, 55 x 55 x 57cm (22 x 22 x 22¾in.), carved terracotta clay with aggregates (fired porcelain).

analytical approach as well as the artistic concerns of meaning and individual expression. She was fortunate to study ceramics at Bath Academy in the mid-1970s during a time of high student/staff ratio under the inspirational guidance of John Colbeck. Much emphasis was put upon learning through discussion rather than through high technical input, and exposure to this breadth of lateral thinking has helped to inform her work both as an artist and educator.

During her final year she started to use coloured clay bodies and learnt how the use of material could transform the final product. Her main preoccupation was in making the form work with the surface through decoration and texture. In the light of her later pioneering research and development, it is significant that Aylieff's emergence as a graduate in the late 1970s coincided with a time of change in the world of ceramics. Allison Britton had introduced a new freedom of form which broke away from the 'brown pot' period of functional throwing enabling studio ceramics to embrace new ideas and concepts.

For the next 14 years Aylieff taught in various art schools but mainly at Bath College of Higher Education where she was responsible for developing and changing the ceramics courses. (She has recently received the accolade of becoming a Professor of Ceramics at the Royal College of Art.) Her work as an educator has paralleled her studio work so that the two have developed symbiotically. Aylieff talks of learning a lot from teaching – of the importance of practising her philosophical ideas about art education through continually challenging the validity of ideas. She says:

> Both my and my students' work needs to be driven by heart and soul but we need to justify what we're doing as we're producing objects from the world's resources.

During this time Aylieff continued developing her investigations begun at college using heavily-stained clays to make vessels that explored the proportions of archetypal form. She talks of the period when she realised a need for change:

> It is a frightening moment when you stand back from your work and see that in many ways you have achieved a certain technical perfection and that the work has reached a point of resolution. For me, what

ensued was much soul-searching and a serious winter of discontent! However, what emerged was the positive recognition for the need to develop alternative ways of working in order to extend and express the nature and range of my ideas and produce more varied solutions. I viewed it very much as a continuation and expansion of the previous work and not a reaction against it.

Over the next two years Aylieff attended the Royal College of Art as a research student, putting herself in the brave position of being taught by her peers. She wanted to explore scale and understand what is meant by sculpture. Part of the research was to find a material both strong enough to make larger pieces and also to be visually exciting. She wanted to release herself from the vertical vessel, to discover new forms without reference to a base or a top. At this point Aylieff had mastered the limitations of working with the vessel, but had no idea of how to deal with sculpture. She thought about the qualities she wanted to develop and realised the need to look at their sources. She was led to the strong articulated lines of early erotic Indian sculpture and to the precision and mathematics of Islamic architecture, which led her back to the symmetry and maths of natural forms such as fruits, seeds and pods. In order to express these ideas Aylieff developed innovative new clay bodies that could be built up into pieces over 1 m (3 ft) high.

> I loosely describe it as a ceramic terrazzo, for it is essentially a composite clay mix that has in its make-up aggregates of glass and ceramic. It is a material that visually reflects my enthusiasm for the surface qualities found in granites, marbles and their conglomerates. Its physical characteristics are those of strength and plasticity, providing the opportunity for the sculptures to be more extravagant in size than might be expected of objects made of clay. When ground and polished, the surfaces are exotically tactile, fragmented with colour, rich and varied in visual texture, with an optical depth enhanced by the inclusions of glass.

Over the next few years as her new work developed it became more about itself than a second reference to its sources. It started to explore internal space with rhythms

(Above) *Bittersweet,* 51 x 51 x 60 cm (20 x 20 x 23½ in.), press-moulded, 2000. Photograph by Steve Yates.

(Opposite) *Swollen Form,* 74 x 74 x 100 cm (29 x 29 x 39½ in.), handbuilt, 2000. Photograph by Sebastian Mylius.

and movements projecting through, as if the enclosed space is pushing and rippling outwards. For this to happen, Aylieff needed to develop a different internal response, a different internal resource than purely translating. To find herself at this point was a huge revelation to her and can be interpreted as a transformation from struggle to a state of effortlessness (the metaphor that springs to mind is a birth after a difficult and prolonged labour).

After detailed planning, original models are carved from styrofoam. Mould divisions are plotted across the surface and the plaster mould is cast – each mould can have up to 10 sections. Some pieces are handbuilt using coiling techniques. Soft clay is pressed into the mould to a thickness of 2 cm (¾ in.), then at leatherhard stage the surfaces are refined with metal scrapers and wooden tools. The piece is allowed to dry very slowly (over 6–8 weeks) to prevent warpage and cracking. Aylieff uses brick clays from Ibstock and a Dutch Vingerling white stoneware clay to which are added fine grogs and/or Molochite (to some but not all the bodies). Body colour comes from commercial stains with a ratio of 17 parts colour to 100 parts clay, and the pitted surfaces are achieved through the addition of combustible

159

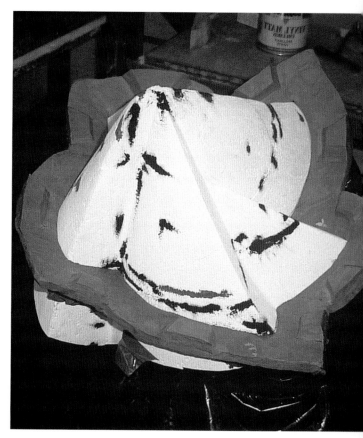

Making sequence

(Above left) Styrofoam model midway through carving using surform blades.

(Above right) Clay strips used to define area to be moulded showing triangular mould location notches.

materials mixed in with the clay. Aggregates include porcelain, coloured fired porcelain, fired terracotta, borosilicate glass and ballotini glass. Firing temperatures vary between clays and are determined by the factors of vitrification temperature, fired body colour, clay strength and durability in order to withstand surface grinding after firing. The fired surface is refined using a water-fed grinding machine that uses diamond pads to polish the surface. Finally the surface is sealed first with a water sealant, then a silicone sealant.

Emmanuel Cooper has talked about Aylieff's work as 'pushing at the boundaries of sculptural form and our understanding of what clay can do'. Aylieff is not interested in using the aggregate material she developed at the Royal College of Art as a 'signature' but is already moving into new territories.

Consciously and unconsciously I'm absorbing and reflecting our time into my work, but when I'm working I'm most concerned with my own interests and preoccupations. I don't feel a part of any particular trends or groupings in craft, art or design. I don't fit into any existing categories in ceramics, such as a functionalist potter or an industrial designer, and I've had to invent my own language for addressing those preoccupations, yet it's a language which people generally seem to understand.

Further reading

'Felicity Aylieff new work, an evolution', published 2000 by Felicity Aylieff

'Felicity Aylieff the Elusive Body', catalogue published by Felicity Aylieff and Bath College of Higher Education

'Larger than Life', by Felicity Aylieff, *Ceramic Review*, no. 165

'Significant Space', Liz Mitchell, *Ceramic Review*, no. 197

Making sequence
(Left) Filling mould with soft clay, 2 cm (¾ in.)
in thickness.

(Below left) Completed mould: sections held together with
metal 'dogs'. Top piece with metal handle for ease of placing
last section.
(Below right) Taking the mould apart to reveal hollow clay
form inside.

Sasha Wardell

Portrait of Sasha Wardell in her studio.
Photograph by Jane Perryman.

(Opposite) Incised pots in the studio.
Photograph by Jane Perryman.

Sasha Wardell has spent over 20 years investigating the properties of slipcast bone china; her concerns are dictated by the limitations and confines of the material and her approach is that of a designer.

Bone china is a very seductive material to work with, possessing qualities of intense whiteness, translucency and strength. It is a very 'single-minded' clay, which forces the maker to work with clarity and precision. Its technical inflexibility and idiosyncratic making and firing characteristics might easily be a deterrent to investigation, but I consider these restrictions and limitations as a challenge to my creativity and working methods.

The work Wardell has developed into a personal vocabulary and style has won her international acclaim and can be instantly recognised as bearing her signature. It expresses qualities associated with the transparency and luminescence of glass combined with the delicacy and weightlessness of an eggshell. It has been described as 'being created by a breath of wind' and has more in common with the elements of light and air than with its origins as earth and bone. Her open vessel forms are graphically crisp and elegant, always springing upwards and outwards from a characteristic narrow base. She says:

I love the juxtaposition of different planes and the challenge of adapting them into a technical confine. I can't cope with wide bases and narrow tops – the proportion doesn't look right.

The openings are often defined by a sloping edge which accentuates this soaring sensation, directing the eye to a higher level as if taking off in an aeroplane or travelling over a suspension bridge.

The characteristics of precision, perseverance and stoicism are basic requirements to achieve success and can often be genetically inherited, each generation adapting them to the appropriate circumstance of their time. It is interesting that Wardell received these qualities from her

father who used them in a very different situation. During our conversation, she told me how he was able to survive as a prisoner of war in Germany by forging passports and identity documents for escapees. It is a dramatic comparison, but vividly illustrates the strength of character needed to persevere and master a difficult material. It is significant that Wardell is one of the few ceramicists to have chosen to work with bone china outside of industry.

With this background it is not surprising that Wardell initially began her degree in graphics at Corsham School of Art. It was not until later that she changed over to ceramics through the guidance of John Colbeck.

Having experienced the early difficulties of controlling clay, the existence of slipcasting was an important discovery as it seemed to provide an alternative to handbuilding and also a means of achieving precise shapes which brought together my ideas about graphic design and ceramics.

Her interest in learning industrial techniques led to an exchange with a course at Limoges in France where she learnt the basics of porcelain painting and mould-making for industry. An industrial MA course at Stoke-on-Trent followed where she was introduced to bone china and began to develop forms which resonated with the architecture of geometrically-based structures.

After college in the mid-1980s Wardell set up a studio in rural Wiltshire. She began investigating the decorative processes of airbrushing coloured glazes onto the surface using illusionist graphics and textiles as inspiration. In the late 1980s Wardell moved to France with her partner where they began a family and restored a farmhouse to run residential ceramics courses. She kept up her English contacts through exhibiting at galleries and craft fairs, but felt isolated and returned to England 10 years later. During the time spent in France her work had not changed and she felt she needed a new challenge. An important change of direction developed whilst taking a part-time Fellowship at Bath College of Art where she began to experiment with layering.

(Above) *Layered and Sliced Bowl*, 16 cm (6¾ in.), 2000. Photograph by Sebastian Mylius.

(Opposite above) *Layered and Sliced Bowl,* 8 cm (3¼ in.), 2001. Photograph by Mark Lawrence.
(Opposite below) *Layered and Sliced Bowls*, 14 cm x 8 cm (5½ x 3¼ in.), 2001. Photograph by Mark Lawrence.

Wardell wanted to bring her pattern-making and forms together to achieve a cohesive whole and also to exploit the translucency of the bone china. She made the decision to abandon glaze:

> The kind of glaze used on bone china gives it a mass-produced industrial look. I realised I could polish down the vitrified surface to get the finish I wanted.

As a result of her investigations she developed a unique 'layering and slicing' technique which creates subtle facets on the outer surface. It involves slicing through three or four coats of different coloured slips to reveal underlying and increasingly transparent layers. At its thinnest point, it is almost possible to see right through.

A plaster cast is taken from the original plaster model which is either formed on the turning lathe or carved directly from a block. The pieces are slipcast in bone china then decorated either through water erosion or slicing and incising techniques. For the slicing process, the pieces are cast in several layers of coloured slips (filling and emptying between layers) and when bone dry a scalpel blade is used to pare down small circles, gradually exposing the underlying layers of slip. An initial soft firing to 900°C (1652°F) is followed by a sanding of the surface to sharpen up the marks before a second firing to 1260°C

Making sequence

(Left) Scalpel blade has been used to pare down small circles which expose the underlying layers of coloured slip. (Right) A loop tool is used to incise marks into the surface at the leatherhard stage.

(2300°F). The incised pieces are worked on at the leather-hard stage using a loop tool to incise marks into the surface, then fired in the same way. Wardell's third decorative technique using water erosion is carried out when the pieces have been removed from their moulds and allowed to dry. Liquitex (a medium for acrylic paints) is painted onto the surface to act as a resist. Next the pieces are gently 'washed' all over with a damp sponge which gradually erodes the unpainted areas. The sponging is done progressively and will determine the thinness of the piece and the depth of relief. Firing is also taken to 1260°C (2300°F).

Within ceramics, it is generally understood that we need to control the material before we can start to let go of it. Most abstract painters began their careers with a thorough grounding in the craft of representational drawing before they became more expressive. Bone china has a strong 'memory' and it took Wardell years to overcome the problems of distortion through the use of setters. She has recently abandoned the setters and begun to explore larger-scale work, allowing the clay's memory its own path of expression. She puts this succinctly:

Once you get to a point, you have to move on.

It is this search for new techniques and directions that keeps Sasha Wardell's work alive and vibrant.

Further reading

'Living Light', Sasha Wardell, *Ceramic Review,* no. 111

Dorothy Feibleman

Dorothy Feibleman has won international acclaim for her mastery of colouring and laminating porcelain. Her highly-refined and distinctive open bowl forms have been achieved through over 30 years of experimentation and investigation. She says:

In 1969, inspired by millefiori glass and ancient miniature glass, I started to work with coloured porcelain. Different coloured porcelains, or different clay bodies are laminated together. Every change in colour, texture or translucency is structural. The

Solo, 'White White Wing' series, base 50 x 50 cm (19¾ x 19¾ in.); bowl 22 x 18 x 15 cm (8¾ x 7 x 6 in.).
Photograph by Studio Tokaname, Japan.

Survival, base 60 x 65 cm (23½ x 25½ in.); bowl 24 x 21 x 14 cm (9½ x 8¼ x 5½ in.). Photograph by Studio Tokaname, Japan.

forms are also dependent on the movement of the different clay bodies during the construction, drying and especially the firing where the movement can be dramatic. All these elements, and their relation to the atmosphere and temperature of the kiln, can be altered to produce very different results using the same materials.

In 1995 I moved to working almost exclusively in white, using up to five structurally similar clays. The whitest porcelain acts as a structure for the more translucent bodies to almost melt within, resulting in textured structural elements with variations in translucency.

Recently Feibleman has been adding chemicals to the laminated clays which cause them to expand during the firing. The black 'wavy' pieces are 'grown' in this way but restricted by moulds in the kiln. As the clay expands against the mould it is forced to change shape but controlled by the pressure of the mould.

David Binns

The minimalist ceramics of David Binns has developed from research exploring aggregate additions to clay bodies. His work is underpinned by an interest in architecture and a knowledge of a range of material disciplines including wood, metals, ceramics and glass which he studied at college. He describes his work:

The experience of working with other materials has been pivotal in informing the way I work with clay. I believe there need be no distinction between the way we respond to different materials – processes and qualities traditionally associated with one discipline, are there to be freely used or adapted for use in another area. This philosophy is intrinsic to my work and is probably one of the most influential ingredients affecting the way I think and make. It is often difficult to fully articulate all the elements that influence my work. Certain influences are obvious, but in truth it is a complex mix of emotions and experiences.

One important source of inspiration was being introduced to traditional Japanese architecture (and from that developing an awareness of Japanese aesthetics and design sensibility). What particularly inspired me was the quality of craftsmanship, attention to detail and a profound sense of order and proportion. I love the use of straight line juxtaposed with the occasional shallow sweeping curve – [similar to] the torii gate. For a number of years I have been making ceramic pieces inspired by architectural form and the phenomena of mathematical repetition. Whilst these issues are important, what has emerged is a desire to 'simplify'. I began to examine closer the idea of 'minimum' and to explore the possibilities that it can offer for working creatively – a process seemingly

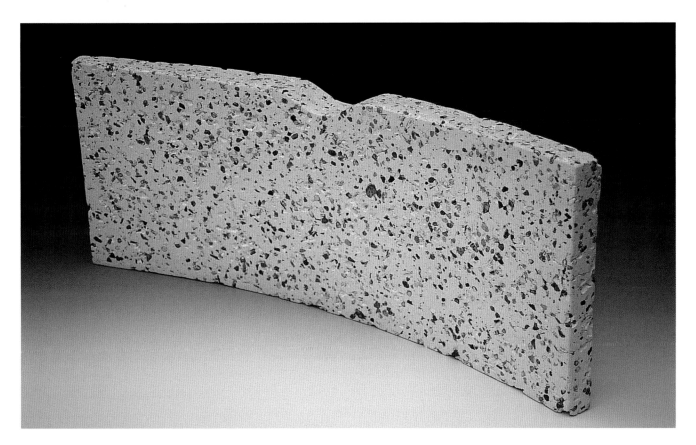

Curved Standing Form, porcelain with pebble aggregate, 66 x 26 cm (26 x 10¼ in.), 2000. Photograph by Dewi Tannatt Lloyd.

easy, but immensely challenging. I like the idea of striving for a quality that can no longer be improved by subtraction. A quality when every detail has been reduced or condensed to the essentials – the result of the omission of unessentials.

I would like to think my work conveys a feeling of calmness or serenity; work that whilst having a distinct presence, would sit quietly and not burden the senses. I am also keen for it to retain a sense of ambiguity of purpose, whilst possibly hinting at some undefined function. The work might vaguely suggest some undefined ritual or ceremony – asking questions yet leaving the viewer free to evolve their own personal interpretation.

Binns works with 'base' bodies such as porcelain and terracottas to which aggregate materials are added by being hand-wedged into the clay. Sometimes the base clay is stained as well with copper or manganese oxides to give extra colour. He uses several different categories of aggregates:

- Coloured grogs made from fired coloured clay and sieved to different sizes.
- Manufactured refractory materials such as molochite, zircon and mullite.
- Naturally occurring granular materials such as granite, flint chippings, fine beach grit, etc.
- Organic or combustible materials which burn out during the firing such as paper pulp, leaves, perlite, wood chips, etc.

The forming methods involve pressing the clay into a plaster mould and the use of wooden and fabric 'formers' to create curved forms. Slow drying over several weeks is necessary because the pieces are thick, followed by an equally slow firing to 1200°C (2192°F). After firing, the pieces are ground with a water-fed diamond grinder and given a light wax polish.

(Left) *Tall Form with Corrugated Face*, terracotta with Molochite, blue and chamotte aggregate, 74 x 23 x 16 cm (29 x 9 x 6¼ in.), 2000. Photograph by Dewi Tannatt Lloyd.

(Opposite) Kiln packed with various clays for firing to make aggregate material. Photograph by Dewi Tannatt Lloyd.

Jeanne Opgenhaffen

Jeanne Opgenhaffen lives and works in Belgium where she has gained international recognition for her explorations into coloured porcelain, using it to produce her own stratigraphy through murals. She has been influenced by landscape and the changing coloration of rock strata.

Her ideas are expressed by recreating the earth's crust from thousands of little porcelain tiles which are overlapped in colour sequences, changing gradually through their hue and tone. Opgenhaffen achieves a strong dialogue between the shadow lines, the open spaces and the denser areas

(Above) *Balance on Lines and Colours,* 83 x 83 cm (32½ x 32½ in.), 2002. Photograph by R. de Wilde.

(Opposite) *Timna Valley,* 100 x 100 cm (39½ x 39½ in.), 1994. Photograph by Milo.

where the colour changes more dramatically, giving a sense of rhythm and movement. The work creates the impression of a dream landscape scored by river-cut channels, breaking open to reveal cracks and fissures where the play of light creates a vibration. The pieces are made from porcelain coloured with oxides, slips and stains, then formed into flat tiles and placed together to form a composition. Firing is to 1200°C (2192°F).

Adrian Knusel

Adrian Knusel is a Swiss ceramicist whose work expresses qualities associated with stone through its mass and surface treatment. Since his training at Corsham College of Art, Knusel has investigated ways to approach clay without the addition of glaze. He discovered grinding as a technique to achieve a rich and tactile surface, and his enclosed containers and open bowl forms have the appearance of granite. In this way, they represent the completed circle of rock eroded to plastic clay and returned to its original state through fire. Knusel successfully combines contrasting properties of precision engineering and organic sensuality in his work; the thrown and highly-turned forms come to life through their surfaces which appear as polished stone and invite handling. He says:

> I wanted a meeting point of when you look at something and when you touch it. I am also concerned with the weight – I wanted to make stones and stone is solid. Some of my work is solid – I wanted to see how thick I could go as an antidote to the striving for thinness and translucency.

Stoneware clay is mixed with copper and cobalt oxides which after the firing and grinding will give it the appearance of granite. Pieces are thrown with thick dense walls and turned, dried slowly and fired to 1260°C (2300°F) in both oxidation and reduction atmospheres.

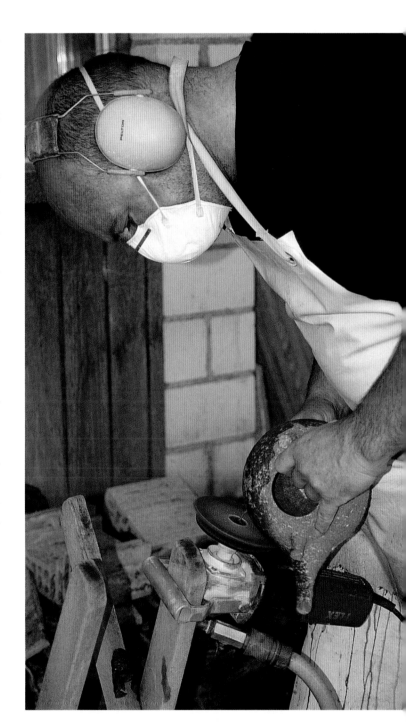

(Opposite page) *Vessel with Stopper*, ht: 75 cm (29½ in.).

(Right) Grinding the surface with a diamond grinder to smooth the surface and reveal the colour from the oxides.
Photograph by Jane Perryman.

Susan Nemeth

Susan Nemeth works with inlaid coloured porcelain to provide pattern and colour in her press-moulded vessel forms. Her interest in pattern originally led her into an exploration of agateware 'loaves' made from different coloured clays which were sliced and rolled flat. She liked the handmade effect achieved by the stretching and distortion of patterns as the designs crept from one layer to another. She describes how she later simplified the process:

> I began to pour coloured slips onto single sheets of clay and applied agate stripes, borders and floral motifs. The idea was transferred into press-moulded bowls, and I liked the way that the design distorted slightly

during press-moulding so that the surface pattern would 'fit' the shape. Decorating both sides involved considering how the flat, decorated sheet would look as a three-dimensional piece. The agates, though, had their limitations and I started to use inlays cut from sheets of coloured clays, which allowed more freedom and control.

For over 20 years Nemeth has been investigating different designs influenced by a wealth of sources, from the paintings of Matisse, Sonia Delaunay and Gillian Ayres to garishly-illustrated cookery books to fabric designs from the 1950s and 1960s. Recently she has used references from Ben Nicholson's paintings of goblets and jugs as well

as his later abstract work, and also the landscape drawings of Paul Klee. She describes her process:

I stain porcelain with combinations of oxides and body stains and roll these coloured clays into thin sheets. I also roll out thin sheets of white porcelain and cover these in thin layers of coloured slips in different combinations: for example I might use black; green and white or blue; red and white or black; brown and white. These sheets are stored in damp conditions and are used for the inlays. A thicker sheet of coloured porcelain is rolled out for the base. Shapes are cut out from the thin sheets of stained or slipped clays and placed on the base, like collage. Sometimes I 'draw' through the layers with a knife to add detail.

When I am happy with the design or image, I turn the whole lot over and roll it flat. Inlays are then added to the reverse side. The pieces are generally press-moulded, although the vases are slab-built using one sheet of clay wrapped around itself. During the process of rolling and press-moulding, the slight distortions create an integral appearance between the surface decoration and the shape. Fired porcelain is the hardest of all clays. It needs no glaze. It is important not to under-fire, to fire the porcelain to its limit, at the point just before bubbling to achieve maximum vitrification and density of colour. During firing the inlays shrink at slightly different rates so that you can see and feel their different levels. Where inlays overlap to form a new colour, this is revealed only after firing. The pieces are buried in saggars full of sand to prevent warping during the firing to 1280°C (2336°F).

Further reading

Ceramic Form; Design and Decoration, Peter Lane, Collins, 1988
Colour in Clay, Jane Waller, Crowood, 1998
'Layer upon Layer', Susan Nemeth, *Ceramic Review*, no. 202
Porcelain, Caroline Whyman, Batsford, 1995

(Left) Porcelain bowl, inlaid with coloured slips and white clays, dia: 24 cm (9½ in.) Photograph by Stephen Brayne.

Claudi Casanovas

Claudi Casanovas is a ceramic sculptor from Catalonia in Spain whose innovative approach to his material has resulted in sculpture which expresses the very essence and energy of clay. It is significant that he began his studies in the theatre. The physical drama of pushing the clay to the edge of destruction remains evident in his work and is celebrated. Tony Birks has said:

Here is a key to his ceramic philosophy or quest; that the potter's materials start in a chaotic state and end, when shaped and decorated, in stability and permanence. His aim is to work somewhere in the middle of this sequence by creating work which is permanent yet essentially unfinished, and by carving before firing and sandblasting afterwards he has both the attitudes and techniques of a sculptor.

Casanovas talks about his work:

I saw someone working at the potter's wheel and I found it magical. After the potter's wheel I tried many methods: biscuit and plaster casts, polyester resin, polyurethane cores, sandjet abrasive spraying of fired pieces, laying coatings of clay upon clay, inducing and simulating cracks and all of these methods obey the primitive instruction first discovered on the wheel: the piece must not be touched; it must be left to grow from inside, as if it were being made by itself, and as if magic were possible.

There comes a moment when I have nothing left but the certainty of what I do not want. I try to deceive myself, I search for a major answer, an ideal stroke; I put all my faith in anything, like a shipwrecked man in an impoverished raft, like a frightened animal for which any little path is a way out. And one after another I start to break up weeks of work, dried pieces and fired alike. I say to myself, 'You're at the beginning, this has already happened to you many times before, you can manage.' And I carry on breaking them, scared as I am. I have

(Above) *Block Form,* ht: 18.5 cm (7¼ in.). Photograph courtesy of Galerie Besson.

(Opposite page) *Rabassa,* 50 x 77 x 54 cm (19¾ x 30½ x 21¼ in.), 2003. Photograph courtesy of Galerie Besson.

nothing left but the certainty of what I do not want. I happen, now and again, to immerse myself in sculptural questions. I never succeed. I always go back to the simple forms and to all the intricacies of fired clay.

The discovery of fire is gradual. Like water, there is no one universal type of fire; sorting out its difficult personalities and approaching them is a slow task. Fire is unpredictable, a border you cannot step over, yet it has the same appeal as the horizon. By firing batches and breaking many a piece you learn to respect it, making an offering with every new batch,

and asking its favour. Fire is always an uncertain ally, never a servant. Clay stops being just a vehicle for water and becomes a register of fire; this is what ceramics is all about.

Casanovas uses many different clays which he mixes with combustible materials and treats with a wide spectrum of processes based on years of unconventional scientific experiments involving heavy machinery. Recent work is formed from blocks of clay which are given their characteristic cracked and eroded texture by partially freezing

them in a large freezer so that the core remains plastic. With the help of a fork lift truck the sections are dropped onto the ground, held together by their plastic core. The block sections are assembled together and then defrosted carefully to avoid collapse. A plaster jacket is cast around the piece, holding it together as it thaws out.

Further reading

Claudi Casanovas, Tony Birks, Marston House, published in association with Galerie Besson, London, 1996.

'Claudi Casanovas', Anna Usborne, *Ceramic Review*, Sep 2003, no. 203

Tina Vlassopulos

Tina Vlassopulos works with burnished vessels which combine organic and rococo forms to set up a dynamic tension between movement and stillness. The twisting extensions which grow from a concave bowl or gourd form create flowing rhythms which lead the eye backwards and forwards across the piece. In contrast, the burnished surface has no colour or tonal variations and expresses restraint and calmness. Vlassopulos has an intuitive approach to her work and has deliberately rejected conceptual references, seeing the development of her work as a personal language: 'my equivalent of writing or talking'. Her pieces can be seen as autobiographical, relating to the emotional and physical experiences in her life; to do with motherhood. There are 'pregnant pots' which are round and centred; 'cuddling pots' where mother and child are connected together; there are pots with a horizontal emphasis to do with feeling tired. She says:

I work on four or five pieces at a time, hopping from one to another. Ideas come from anywhere and at unexpected moments. Sometimes one idea leads to another. The most satisfying and consuming part of the process is inventing a new shape and so I tend to build new pieces very quickly. I use either terracotta or white stoneware clay mixed with T-Material and add various oxides to give the body colour: cobalt carbonate for blue; chrome and copper carbonate for green; and a mixture of terracotta and white stoneware for the sienna colour. Each form is begun by press-moulding a bowl shape, then adding coils which are supported with different shaped sponges. Sometimes one part has to dry sufficiently before adding another part on. To avoid cracking I score and apply a vinegar slip between each coil. Then comes an awful lot of scraping using Surform blades, metal kidneys and wooden ribs to achieve a smooth surface. After burnishing, the pieces are fired to 920°C (1688°F).

(Opposite page) *Pot with Scroll,* l: 32 cm (12½ in.), 1999.
Photograph by Mike Abrahams.

180

Index